Sports Psychology Basics

by Andrew Caruso

REEDSWAIN PUBLISHING

What coaches are saying about
Sports Psychology Basics :

"Having been around athletes and teams as a player and coach his entire life, Coach Caruso began using sports psychology long before it was fashionable. Sports Psychology Basics is a practical guide: A must for all serious athletes and coaches. Andy makes us realize how important goal setting, imagery and relaxation techniques are in the mental development of all athletes. This is a valuable resource!"
Dagan Nelson, Assistant Men's Basketball Coach at Eastern Kentucky University: Former; NYU Assistant, Head Coach Melbourne Central Catholic, Five Star Instructor, player at Ramapo College of New Jersey.

"This book is a great tool for youth and high school athletes. It is simple to read for student athletes and would help their mental game in any sport. Coaches also benefit and get a better understanding of what goes through young athletes' minds during competition and practices. Andrew Caruso has done a great job in his research and this is a must read for all athletes and coaches."
Ted Dent, Washington Capitals Hockey Video Coach, pro player East Coast League and Division I St. Lawrence college player.

"This book fills a huge void in the world of coaching; the need for a rational, researched, practical approach to sports psychology goes beyond the 'winning is everything' and 'do whatever it takes to win' mentality. An intelligent alternative! A model the player can use that can be applied to all aspects of life, long after playing days are over. Some of what came naturally to Magic Johnson, Larry Bird, Zinedine Zidane, Roberto Carlos, Tiger Woods and others has been revealed by Andy's informative and insightful style. I expect players and coaches of all sports to benefit greatly form this book. A required reading for all coaches and athletes."
J.C. Lydon, MD, licensed soccer coach and administrator for 14 years, high school basketball coach for 2 years.

"The important role that the mental side of sport plays in athletic success has become a major topic of discussion over the past 5 years. Athletes in individual sports such as golf and tennis have been at the forefront of this modern thinking. To date, less has been written about the practical skills of the mental development of team sports, so Andy's excellent treatment brings a team perspective to a very important topic in modern day athletic development. These skills transfer well to business because it requires composure, focus and teamwork."
Chris Price, Business, President of Xara Sportswear, former Soccer Industry Council of America President and youth coach.

Library of Congress Cataloging - in - Publication Data

Sports Psychology Basics
Caruso, Andrew

ISBN No. 1-59164-083-0
Lib. of Congress Control Number 2004095425
© 2004

Art Direction, Layout and Proofing
Bryan Beaver

Printed by
DATA REPRODUCTIONS
Auburn, Michigan

Reedswain Publishing
562 Ridge Road
Spring City, PA 19475
800.331.5191
www.reedswain.com
info@reedswain.com

CONTENTS

ACKNOWLEDGEMENT

To all the aspiring athletes, coaches and people who see sport as a vehicle for developing character and values that contribute to a better and more productive life.

In the end, the greatest acknowledgement goes to all the players, both young and adult, that I have had the opportunity to teach. Their hard work and the lessons both learned and taught are a wonderful reward.

They have helped me to see how years later the lessons on the field and in the gym paid great dividends. They have all given much more to me than I could ever hope to give to them.

To entrust young people to another is a courageous act of faith in human nature. Parents and players have given great trust to coaches. One only hopes that their faith is fulfilled. Thanks to all the schools, their athletic directors and principals, clubs and state associations that have allowed me coaching and playing opportunities.

Even the humbling thought that someone would take the time to grow in this domain by reading this book is a compliment to all of you. None-the-less I am greatly indebted to Richard Diedrichsen who is much more than an editor of this work. He has given me the courage to proceed and offered encouragement and advice all along the way.

I thank you, the reader, for this opportunity. I hope that some thoughts and activities will become a part of your playing, coaching, and ultimately, your life skills.

Thank you.

Great athletes often say things such as "I could see it all happening," "I could feel it," or "I just was in a zone so it seemed to happen by itself." This book is about what virtually all sports greats possess beyond their physical ability. Now that the science of sports psychology understands those characteristics, they are transferable to young athletes with the desire to achieve long and short range goals, focus, and mental toughness.

This text is aimed at athletes and coaches. Virtually all coaches agree that the mental game is the number one element in consistent high level achievement in sports, yet so little time is devoted to it. Here is your chance to incorporate the mental game into your actual practices. Your program will surely benefit, and the positive long range results will help to remind you why you were intrigued with coaching (teaching) in the first place!

While many of the texts on the market serve a useful purpose, this simple, clear and concise text is geared to youth and high school players and their coaches! Many college and professional coaches and players can also garner much from it. The basic theory and the actual techniques are clarified, along with specific examples in a myriad of individual and team sports.

With space and lines for you to add your own personal touches to the activities, this book becomes an extremely useful workbook that can actually be used in the gym or at the field. In short, it is practical and detailed. Coaches may want every player to have his or her own copy to individualize his or her goals, according to individual personality, temperament, role or position on the team, etc.

Enjoy this book. Try a few activities and see the results immediately. Naturally the more you practice the skills, the more adept you will become. Consequently, greater and greater benefits will accrue, not only in athletics but also in all facets of life, from the battlefield to the boardroom, from the courtroom to the schoolroom, and even from the construction site to the anthropology dig.

Just like your sport, much of it is the journey, but we all know that journeys carried out with an excellent plan, hard work and commitment lead to excellence. Now you can enjoy the journey and the results!

INTRODUCTION
Sports Psychology: Why We Need It and How It Can Help Us

Probably since the beginning of organized sports, coaches have made comments like these, whether they are fact or fiction:

* "One of their parents said they should win because we are a weak team."

* "They are a skillful team, so we have to be physical, tackle hard, and have an attitude!"

* "This is a dirty team, so play accordingly."

* "You guys look dead today! You're just asking for a loss! Get with it, or go home now!"

* "Joann, your last game was awful, don't go out and repeat it today."

* "Joann, you had a great game last week, so just go out and do it again!"

Coaching this way is not only ineffective, but also inappropriate. The "Win one for the Gipper" speech sounds good in old movies, but does not work with most young athletes and teams today. Indeed the above approaches are from the same era and mentality that denied young players a drink of water in the hopes of "toughening them up."[1] Nowadays we know better than to withhold something our players need, whether that something is physical, mental, or ethical.

Recent advances in the science of psychology have revealed what coaches and players need in developing what some call "mental toughness" or a "winning attitude."[2] These advances recognize the high level of competitiveness in present day athletics and the millions of females involved as fully as males at all levels of sport. As a response to these advances, this book fills a major gap in coaching: it not only illustrates how the psychological component of sports is just as important as the

1. Hydration needs to be understood as a need of at least 24 hours before rigorous training and matches.
2. Mental Toughness is defined by these skills. Being "soft" is the lack of these skills.

physical, technical, and tactical components; it also gives coaches and players the tools and proven techniques to enhance individual and team performance in training and competition.

While no amount of sport psychology will take the place of quality training, intrinsic motivation, and interpersonal relationships with players, research clearly shows that adding the science of sport psychology to these basics will dramatically improve the three key ingredients to a successful athletic program: fun, participation, and development. In fact, sport psychology is the glue that holds these three ingredients together.

Thus, an entirely new approach to coaching fun, participation, and development!

Research consistently indicates that youth and high school athletes play sports mainly for the fun of it. While not researched greatly, this is probably true for every age. Coaches must therefore maintain this priority if they expect their players to continue in the sport. Generally, participation drops 50% between the ages of 10 and 14, whether the activity is sports, music, dance, or whatever. While most youngsters find other interests or choose to specialize in fewer activities, many simply leave because it is no longer fun.

Therefore the motive for playing or coaching a sport depends heavily on enjoyment and success. Players who participate for the pure enjoyment of the sport are intrinsically motivated, as opposed to extrinsically motivated players, who play mainly for their parents, social prestige or for other external reasons. Intrinsically motivated players have better attendance, fitness, nutrition and rest. Most importantly, they are willing to put in the countless hours required to develop athletic excellence. At the same time they are far less likely to burn out!

In youth and high school sports, burnout is often misunderstood. When young athletes lose interest, they often cite spending too much time on a sport as the cause. But the real reason is more likely lack of enjoyment, which is not simply a lack of fun, but also the lack of participation or development.[3]

---

3. The desire to learn consistently scores very high when players give reasons for engaging in sport.

If burnout came from just doing too much of something, there would never be outstanding artists, musicians, athletes, attorneys, doctors, architects, etc. Virtually all highly accomplished people spend an enormous amount of time perfecting themselves, but find ways to enjoy the challenge and subtleties of their craft.

But there are also compelling social benefits for athletes who play for the fun of it: they develop better social relationships, sportsmanship and other fair play notions as long as their coaches also value these ideas.

The idea of fair play brings us to another area of sports that is often confusing. Sports psychology includes developing "mental toughness," but it clearly distinguishes between aggression and assertiveness. Aggression which intends to hurt someone can never be a part of sports. Assertiveness, on the other hand, aims at getting the job done and winning the contest within the rules and spirit of the game. While every sport has its own examples of assertive versus aggressive behaviors, it all comes down to intent. Even intending to get the ball and hurting the opponent at the same time is simply not acceptable.

The distinction between aggression and assertiveness is extremely clear for all moral athletes who compete very hard, while maintaining the athletic task as the goal, and never setting out to hurt someone. Mental toughness, then, is not sheer aggression. This distinction again goes back to appropriate motivation.

It is very difficult, if not impossible, for players or coaches to benefit from sports participation if they begin with an inappropriate motive. While it is laudable to coach because someone is needed, it is far more satisfying to coach for the love of the sport and the potential values that sport can offer. These values enhance the skills of sports psychology, and are likely to carry over to high-level performance in other life pursuits. For instance, establishing and pursuing clear goals and measuring progress toward those performance goals is great for any career, business venture, organization or boardroom.

Another valuable skill is learning self-control in volatile competitive environments. Often learned on athletic fields, this becomes a great asset years later in personal, family and professional life. Composure in

3

chaotic and emergency situations saves self-esteem, careers, relation-ships, even lives!

The lack of self-control, though triggered by desire to win, actually contributes more to defeat than to victory! When coaches and players lose their mental and emotional focus, their performance suffers. Of course, so does their enjoyment. In surveys, children frequently blamed this over-emphasis on winning as their main cause for quitting. While the desire to win can be a positive influence toward gaining excellence, we all know that valuing winning at all costs ruins fun, participation, and development, the very foundations of youth athletics. Therefore, coaches and players would do well to act as if they had to watch their performance on videotape after each game. In general terms, not only with players from age 5 - 12, but also up through the junior varsity level in high school, the emphasis must be on learning the sport and develop-ing the individual players.

To get the best from their players and themselves, coaches should learn the basic sports psychology science as contained in this book. The fabricated notions of previous eras have unpredictable effects on play-ers. For example, a coach may think that a player needs to be psyched up, when in fact the player may really need to be calmed down. Or the coach may think that another player needs to be calmed down when in fact she can only perform well when at a very high arousal level. Surprisingly, team talks in this realm are almost always destructive, since virtually all teams have some players of each type. Generally, about 75% of your players need to be given relaxation cues as opposed to motivational psyche-up data. Therefore, a simple/clear game plan that was rehearsed, instead of a "Let's get fired up!" diatribe, will be much more beneficial to your team.

Modern sports psychology begins with telling the simple truth in a reasonably positive manner. Naturally it is best to focus on and discuss more of the positive, like reminding the team of its real assets. This is not to ignore correction, but the great preponderance of correct-ing should take place in training, rather than before or during games. How does a coach make the truth simple? By having a cognitive game plan; that is, by focusing on what was trained for that week. This helps to avoid some problems of poor home hip pocket psychology, as shown in the familiar quotations above.

One of the many benefits of this sports psychology program is fewer parent problems, whether it is a club or school program. Anyone who questions your methods has a difficult time making a case when your program represents state-of-the-art practices of the foremost sports psychology experts and the best coaches. These practices are nothing more than the methods used by great coaches such as John Wooden. And for your own satisfaction, you know that the values built into your program carry over to other life activities. Using these guidelines, you are never damaging the child's ego, as is often the case with homespun personal psychology. This fringe benefit can grow into a valuable skill as the coach uses sports psychology to become a better motivator, teacher and communicator. This is the very essence of leadership.

The era has passed when one can operate a program that is untested and totally subjective. The era of "do what I say, not what I do" has also passed. Today's coach cannot escape being a role model. Whether coaches are aware of it or not, their players are influenced by the coaches' behavior.

While everything you do is suited to your style, time frame and your point of view, this approach in no way hampers your creativity. It is based upon firm scientific theory and practical application as prescribed by authorities and endorsed by elite athletes.

And it works! Countless success stories attest to the effectiveness of sports psychology. Mitch Kupchak, a ten-year NBA player and general manager of the L.A. Lakers often credited Stan Kellner, author of *Living the Miracle*, for his success. Kellner helped Mitch develop a long range plan of coaching through junior high and high school. In a single season, Brentwood High went from a perennial 5-10 game winner to a consistent county champion on Long Island, an area with a long history of talent and team parity that has produced many NBA players. Kellner's emphasis on "Yes, I can!" sport psychology and clarity of player responsibilities was instrumental to this accomplishment.

I personally know a gentleman, let's call him Dick, who interviewed for a job in a school known for outstanding academic achievement, but not athletics. An extraordinary number of students entered prestigious colleges, but the football team had not won a game in three years. Dick claimed that he would win the league championship in his first year, explaining that the intellectual assets of the students were not being utilized in the football program. Once hired, he instilled a winning mentality, carried out well planned skill sessions, capitalized on the team's intellectual strengths and minimized their deficits. The team did win the championship that year, with a pass to a tight end standing in the end zone all by himself. Cunning strategy proved itself useful even in a game as physical as football!

How does sports psychology work? Research strongly suggests that 10% is achieved by the conscious mind and 90% by the unconscious. **But it is the conscious mind that programs the unconscious mind.** Sports psychology has discovered various techniques for accomplishing this. While this is easy to say, it is difficult to attain and requires a very concerted effort; the unconscious is so wrapped up in self-image that it is difficult to perform much above the self-image level.

Thus, sport psychology is constantly attempting to be positive and thus raise the self-image, in regard to the individual's sport, and also the whole person. High performance will not result from physical practice alone, though without question physical practice is an absolute necessity, and a key ingredient for any sport.

While the complex integration of the conscious and unconscious mind is not fully understood at this time, the two constantly play on one another. We see this in the way the human brain functions. The left brain is analytical and useful to perfecting technique, while the right brain is more able to take the entire action in one continuous whole. In the early stages of learning a physical skill, the athlete is using the left brain - analytical, well thought out, and technical. But once that skill is mastered, she must let go of all the details that have been practiced mentally and physically and now simply *let it happen*. The athlete is moving into feeling and seeing the end performance result of the moment. She simply goes with the flow!

The connection of the physical and mental works in both directions, thus increasing performance exponentially! For example, the early stages of re-programming the mind to "accentuate the positive, eliminate the negative" requires a bit of role-playing, like being an actor. An effective cue for this technique is to "act as if." Since you may not feel

extremely confident in your skills, you may have to pretend for a prolonged period of time, as you work to master both the mental and physical skills. Part of the mental training, then, starts with the physical
expressions of confidence: an upright posture, a smile, and a strong
voice. Experts suggest that it may take six weeks to realize significant
progress in this area. But as you simultaneously work on your physical
skills, improvement is certain. As Maxwell Maltz, one of the "fathers of
sports psychology" puts it: "We fake it until we make it!". By this,
Maltz does not mean lying to oneself, he is simply promoting having a
positive outlook and viewing oneself as having positive performances.

Obviously, athletic training embodies physical training. Here too,
sports psychology can offer insights. On his "TeamMastermind" website, Samuel Hershberg discusses the "Law of 21," an idea based on
research indicating that 21 repetitions of something will generally make
it permanent or place it in the unconscious mind. Additional repetitions
may be of great help at crunch time. In any case there must be an abundance of repetitions of the techniques presented in this book. Review
and repetition is always a part of maintaining skill, whether that skill is
physical or mental.

"You play the way you practice!" Every coach and athlete knows
that this is true in physical practice. But not all realize that it is just as
true (and as important) in mental rehearsal. Therefore, some sports psychology must be done in the gym, at the field, on the courts in order to
integrate the physical training with the power of the mind.

While some of this may sound complex, the method is quite similar
to developing any physical skill; we create a series of proven steps or
building blocks and work from that foundation. We concentrate on one
thing at a time, and gradually learn to put all the elements together.
Remember that if you put good stuff in, good stuff will come out. The
simple affirmation of "Yes I can" is extremely helpful for attaining positive final results.

The essence of today's sports psychology is long and short-range
goal setting, assessment, visualization, imagery, simulation, focus, refocus, relaxation exercises, flow replication, and motivation - the contents
of this manual. This information completes and complements the typical
athletic program of fitness, technical, and tactical training. If your pro-

gram fully develops the necessary fitness, technical and tactical skills, then it is time to incorporate *Sports Psychology Basics* into your training. It is all you will need to bring you to the next level of your game - the level of champion!

The Athlete's Journal

Many great athletes keep journals, especially in golf, tennis and bowling, but also in many team sports. Journal writing is a very powerful tool for the athlete or coach of any sport or any team. Some journal entries may be intended for another reader, perhaps the coach, a captain, teammate, or trainer. Other entries may be kept confidential, and used as a very personal/internal activity, a conversation with one's self.

In either case, there are many benefits to journal writing. Simply focusing on the journal requires in-depth thinking and raises awareness. Through the journal, athletes can reflect on their experiences and consider new perspectives. Journals also help the athlete avoid previous mistakes and sort out numerous other problems, such as fear of failure or relationships with the coach and team. Questions for meditation by the player are frequently an excellent technique to allow the player to overcome a problem. But most of all, the journal facilitates duplicating previous success. In short, the athlete's journal is a versatile tool that aids every area of sports psychology and general athletic performance.

The coach also can benefit when players trust him with their personal experiences and feelings through the journal. Often players are willing to say in writing what they are reluctant to say out loud. The person who seems to be losing interest in practice may reveal that his family may have to move out of the area. Another player may reveal a history of bad feelings between himself and a teammate. Of course, such information must be kept confidential, but it helps the coach to understand the players' individual situations. Simply showing a bit of understanding and support may be enough to lighten the player's burden.

Despite all these benefits, even athletes who practice other sport psychology techniques may not take advantage of journal writing. Most have a sort of "mental journal" and more or less clear goals in their mind. Many believe that they can accomplish excellence without the help of tools such as journals to achieve their real potential. But these short-cuts generally are not nearly as effective. Journals are a proven way for athletes to set and revise goals, assess their progress, ask themselves important questions and thereby open up their inner wisdom.

A few hints on making a journal most valuable are in order. Certainly a calm, quiet, solitary place will allow for proper concentration. Dating entries is important for assessment, goal setting, future reference and for other readers. As for how often the athlete should write in the journal, one or two total entries are unlikely to accomplish much. On the other hand, daily entries might be very productive, but unrealistic for some athletes and whoever else reads the journal. Possibly three to five entries a week during the season is appropriate and realistic, but should include thoughts on practice performance as well as games. Finally, the athlete or coach should maintain a positive tone that builds confidence; going back and re-reading many positive journal entries is a great way to maintain your motivation!

The athlete's journal should have questions, exclamations, cue words, objects for focusing, relaxation monologues, drawings, charts, or whatever will help her performance. If teammates are willing to share their journals by all means do an exchange. Of course, some athletes just like to keep their journal exclusively for their own use or as a dialogue with the coach.

Sheila Bender in her book *Keeping a Journal You Love* claims that the more one journals, the more he becomes accepting of himself. She reminds us that journals do not require perfect spelling, punctuation or grammar; but technical details or date and time references and the like can be valuable, since the journal must be understood by the writer and possibly referred to at a later date. Ultimately, journals are a place to capture valuable ideas, the creative spirit and the essence of a person's desires.

Probably the most effective techniques for creating self-confidence and a positive effective sports psychology are the ones that you create. Your journal can be the source and archive for these techniques. To personalize your own program, try these journal activities, or let them serve as a springboard for your own ideas.

♦ Make a list of at least three of the positive things you have accomplished, or all the successes you have had in all your life experiences aside from sports.

_____

_____

_____

_____

_____

♦ Using the above list, now make a list of five things that you think have enabled you to achieve those successes; in other words, your strengths (as a person, not just an athlete), things that have gained you recognition or are simply wonderful things that people have said or written about you.

_____

_____

_____

_____

_____

_____

♦ Now think carefully and list the five greatest strengths that you have in your sport. Everyone has made an excellent pass, serve or play at one time or another; you may have done this more often that you realized. Possibly you want a teammate or friend to give you what he/she thinks are your greatest strengths. Or give a file card to your coach and have him/her list your strengths. Coaches, list your coaching strengths.

_____

_____

_____

_____

_____

_____

- List three ways how you turned a negative event into a positive, first as a person and then three more as an athlete or coach.

_____

_____

_____

_____

_____

_____

_____

Clear goals maximize all the time you spend on your sport.

- Write in your journal or a single file card the five most important things you will do in the next six months to attain your peak performance.

_____

_____

_____

_____

_____

_____

- Write down the three best things about your role model and choose which one or two is most important in improving your own abilities.

_____

_____

_____

_____

_____

_____

_____

- Pay close attention to the responses of champions interviewed on television or in sports articles, and note how they consistently feel that in the future they can overcome adversity or repeat excellence. Though it may appear that they are finding excuses for a poor per-formance, in reality they nearly always think, "I can fix it." And, of course, champions frequently do; that is why they are champions. Write down an example from a professional and a case of your own where you 'self-prophesized' and it really happened.

_____

_____

_____

_____

_____

_____

_____

_____

_____

- List five things in your sport that **YOU** are in total control over. (You can control other things besides heartbeat, breathing, muscle relaxation, and focus.) All this will build your sense of well-being, or in the words of Stan Kellner, your *'Power State'*.

_____

_____

_____

_____

_____

_____

_____

_____

_____

- Describe how you would change any of the following to a more powerful and positive posture: your tone of voice, posture, facial expression, hand positioning, body movement, especially your walking gate, eye contact, dress, hair style, maybe even footwear for health and comfort.

_____

_____

_____

_____

_____

_____

_____

_____

_____

_____

- Mentally "go to a place" that really made you feel that you were in a power state. Describe that place and the sense of power you feel.

_____

_____

_____

_____

_____

_____

_____

_____

_____

_____

_____

_____

_____

_____

- Find an area each day that will provide a few moments of solitude in order to do your visualizations, read your goals or cue words or any of the mentally strengthening techniques that you have chosen to employ. List when and where:

_____

_____

_____

_____

_____

_____

_____

_____

_____

_____

As a coach assigning journal entries to players, there are several issues confronting you. First of all, are you going to read some or all of the players' journal entries? It is recommended that the coach read and discuss at least some of these journal entries on a regular basis. The coach could have two or three mandatory collections of the journal and then a few voluntary collections. It is further recommended that the coach speak privately with the writer rather than in front of the whole team; yet there may be times when an open forum is beneficial.
In any case, players need to know beforehand if their writing will be read, if it will be discussed, and if so whether the discussion will take place individually or in the group. Certainly, it is crucial that the coach avoid hurting any player's feelings by criticism. Neutral commentary or even a question written in the player's journal by the coach is often the best choice! Let the individual sort it out. Furthermore, athletes should be protected from having teammates read their journals without their permission.

For a coach monitored journal, the underlined items in this list are recommended, but coaches should feel free to choose what best suits their needs:

- Journal reader (<u>discusses some</u>/does not discuss any) entries with writer.
- Journal reader discusses items in journals with (<u>individual</u>/whole team.)
- Journal (reader/<u>writer</u>) selects topics except initial goal setting entries.
- Topics are (very narrowly defined/<u>more open ended</u>).
- Topics are (limited/<u>not limited</u>) to the sport.
- Entries (must be shared/<u>can be voluntarily shared</u>) with team.
- Reader (<u>may sometimes provide</u>/never provides) a consensus of players' thoughts.
- Coach (<u>provides writing time at practice</u>/ assigns journal writing for player's own initiative).
- Journal entries (must have/<u>do not need</u>) formal sentence structure.

CHAPTER 1
Goal Setting

How many times have we witnessed a scene like this? A youth team was playing well enough to be ahead 1-0 in a soccer match at half-time. During the break, the well-meaning youth coach emphasized the trophy they would get if they won the game. He focused solely on the outcome (the trophy). He ignored the opportunity both to reinforce what the team had been doing well and to explain where they needed to improve. The fixation on the outcome goal largely contributed to the team's loss of a winnable match. Discussing the game plan or strategies that had been practiced in the last session would be of much greater value, not only on that game day, but also for long term development.

While the coach knew that setting goals is an important step to success, this was the wrong time for an outcome goal. Outcome goals may be suitable for the long-range, but <u>performance goals are the necessary steps in accomplishing that long-range goal</u>. Performance goals could well have produced a positive outcome to the game. But even if the team still lost, at the very least they may have learned something very useful to improve future performances. Goals based on outcomes usually create nothing but negative feelings when those outcomes are not reached. In fact, only 10% of goals should be outcome goals.

In addition to being performance-based, goals should be specific, measurable, and limited in number. The coach can model this procedure by setting the team goals with input from the players. A good practice is to write down the team goals and distribute them to each player, perhaps showing how the goals are performance-based, specific, measurable, and limited in number for any given moment of time. Throughout the season, the coach and team can regularly review and revise these goals.

Players should write down their individual goals in a journal and turn them in to the coach periodically. The coach should consider responding positively and offering further insights into items in the player's journal.

Players can formulate their personal goals in categories of time, starting with the longest term goal, a "dream goal" for the highest eventual level, such as committing to a Division I college sport or making the high school varsity team in sophomore year, etc.

Follow this with a clear, definitive **annual goal**, or perhaps a seasonal goal. For example, "I want to be able to serve a ball 4 out of 5 times into a three yard circle from a distance of 25 yards. Also I want to get 4 out of 5 shots on goal, or I want to lose no more than a single 1 versus 1 situation per game."

Next is a **monthly goal** which could be "I want to have at least 50% of all my crosses playable by my intended receiver."

A **weekly goal** might be "I want to perfect my 1 v 1 dribbling move of inside/outside of the foot to the point that I can beat Mary (my frequent partner in 1 v 1 exercises) 3 times out of 5 attempts."

A **daily goal**, if one is decided upon, could be "I want to try to receive 60 air balls today from 20 yards away and control the ball 4 out 5 times to within 3 yards of me, putting some in front, left and right of my body."

Notice that the above goals are measurable <u>performance</u> goals. While striving to be an All-League or All-State player is a worthy goal (these are <u>outcome</u> goals), the most important question is "how do I achieve this?" One reason that outcome goals alone are not as valuable as performance goals is that they do not define what is needed to attain them. Furthermore, an athlete may be more than worthy of All-League but simply not chosen by the selecting body. The progress toward such goals (whether achievement failed or succeeded) should be noted in one's journal. To what extent one succeeded or failed is critical. Plans for what must be done to achieve the goal completely can also be written in the journal. For example, "What sub-components can I accomplish in the next two practice sessions?"

In actual practice, the goals may be ever changing, but the athlete is constantly trying to find a way to attain the bigger more complete goal. Coaches should use the achievable sub-goals to constantly offer encouragement and positive reinforcement toward reaching higher performances.

In short, great success is obtained one step at a time, following a careful plan (clear goals). If time and conditions permit, the coach can help players individually in setting their goals. At the college and professional level, where a coach is a full-time professional, this is virtually always done.

To place goal setting in a larger psychological context, research clearly indicates that people who work toward both long and short-term goals are happier than those who only dream about long-term goals like winning the lottery or becoming a movie star. The difficulty in sensing any progress toward those long-term goals leads to inertia. However, the feeling that one is working positively toward her short-term goals certainly contributes to success, and at the same time brings those long-term goals closer. Therefore, we need both short and long-term goals to be happy or successful.

In short, goal setting needs to be done regularly, even daily, using these principles:
1. both short term and long term
2. performance based
3. challenging, yet realistic
4. measurable
5. using strategies to overcome obstacles
6. generating and accepting feedback
7. establishing and fine-tuning target dates
8. frequently reassessed and adjusted

◆ Use the lines below for your various long-range goals and some portion of your seasonal goals:

_____

_____

_____

_____

_____

_____

_____

_____

_____

_____

_____

_____

_____

_____

_____

_____

_____

_____

_____

_____

_____

_____

_____

_____

_____

_____

_____

_____

_____

_____

_____

_____

_____

_____

_____

_____

You will learn more about the details of short range and daily goals later on in this manual.

A familiar scenario which is common in high school basketball involves early arriving players shooting from half court and beyond. They may be improving slightly on their low-percentage desperation shot, but it seldom determines game results. Besides, shooting off balance and using poor form may be hurting their regular 3-point shooting technique! If these players knew more about goal setting and its corollary, assessment, they would realize that practicing a typical 3-point shot or even a foul shot would be of greater value. With a little further knowledge, they would develop the techniques that virtually guarantee improvement in these areas.

Setting goals and practicing various sports psychology techniques is only the beginning. Without careful monitoring and evaluation your results will be spotty at best. This is what assessment is all about. Too many athletes and coaches regard assessment as an after-thought deserving only a casual or occasional review. But because assessment is a highly individual area, it requires a great deal of self-searching and concentration. Every individual is different, and must decide what kinds of physical practice and mental strength programs will work best for her goals. The value of these individual efforts and goal-setting preparations for regular training sessions should never be underestimated.

Once goals are set, how do we go about achieving them? The answer lies in assessment. Assessment is simply measuring the degree of success in achieving these goals; therefore, it is what makes goal-setting productive! Most goals must have very specific assessments as well as constant monitoring with very clear and detailed evaluation criteria. The idea is to have very small but definite and measurable increments of progress. As you succeed in each small part of your game you are constantly getting better and gaining in confidence. At the same time assessment helps to make clearer and better goals.

Most of the assessment has to be done by the individual athlete. Still, nearly all coaches and even teammates are ready to help if asked. If you listen to your coach carefully you may find that he/she makes valuable suggestions in the training sessions. Teammates may not be able to prescribe assessments, but they are more than capable of offering opinions or physical assistance with what is self-prescribed. Coaches may be able to help athletes in developing their program of progress assessment.

Assessment involves an awareness of the three basic levels of challenge in completing a technical or tactical task: independent, instructional and frustration levels. At the independent level an activity is too easy; the player can already achieve the task nearly 100% of the time or with little effort. At the other end of the spectrum, frustration level results from a goal that is too ambitious (difficult) <u>at the moment</u> and virtually guarantees failure.

The desired goal for nearly all training is the instructional level, at which the player can accomplish the task the vast majority of the time with great effort; this level provides skill development and confidence building. Since the player experiences some failure, particularly when effort and focus are lacking, the task provides a healthy balance of challenge and success.

That balance differs according to the type of skill being practiced. For tactical (decision making) activities an appropriate percentage is about 66% (success 2 out of 3 times). For technical (basic skills) practice the suggested percentage can be 80% or even 90%, which minimizes the incorrect repetition of a skill. This destroy one's confidence. Hence, it allows for steady growth.

Obviously with a completely new skill, difficult environmental conditions, after a severe loss that has shaken confidence, or numerous other circumstances, judgment and flexibility should moderate the percentage guidelines. Especially in such cases, the coach should not rush to a hasty assessment, but allow players sufficient time to practice the skill in question, while offering correction and encouragement.

After each assessment it may be necessary to raise the bar, lower it, change it somewhat or even completely. Assessment procedures must be pertinent to very short-term, intermediate and long-range goals. Simply said, assessment allows one to be extremely efficient in goal setting!

To see how this works in practice, let's look at some examples. A golfer may want to drop 12 foot putts 90% of the time. He can do this from 6 feet with 90% accuracy. He therefore extends his distance to 7 feet and continually extends his distance as he achieves the 90% goal. If he falls into the 60% range when he reaches 10 feet he will move back to nine feet or temporarily accept the low percentage of achievement. In most cases it is best to return to high conversion options.

The concept of instructional level is critical to both the player and coach because it greatly facilitates steady progress. Naturally the coach is always attempting to plan, and during practice adjust to a steady progress level. In fact, this is one of the elements of excellence. This may be one of the pivotal reasons why John Wooden spent 2+ hours of planning for every 1 hour of practice. Frequently this time was spent not by him alone, but with his entire staff! There is no need to indicate the talent he made available to UCLA, especially since he won many championships. However, he also won championships without a true center, which was unheard of in his era. Much of that planning time was undoubtedly devoted to instructional level and assessment!

General Assessment Areas:

- **Timing:** X distance in Y amount of time: how much time needed to score a goal by dribbling from midfield and firing a shot from the 18 yard line. Assess a month later after you have established your present standard.
- **Measurable distance, height, speed, weight:** Vertical jump, speed of your pitch, serve or kick; weight you can press, etc.
- **Percentage of success:** pitches in strike zone, foul shots, slap shots, penalty kicks, successful serves, bowling strikes from ten attempts, etc.
- **Time spent on solo practice perfecting individual skills:** on days off, or before or after practice.
- **Time spent on sports psychology techniques.**

The number and variety of assessments is obviously unlimited. Be creative and feel free to ask teammates, parents, coaches, managers and anyone knowledgeable about your sport how you can assess your progress. Avoid those who are merely subjective or who have provided poor recommendations in the past.

If you fail at a particular skill, simply attempt to adjust the goal or give yourself more time to achieve it. In this way there really won't be any failure, but only the need to find increments and methods for progress! Revel in small accomplishments, because a Michael Jordan, Tiger Woods, Joe DiMaggio, Anika Sorenstam, Pele, Mia Hamm, Joe Montana, Wayne Gretzky, or Serena Williams was never developed in a week, month or even a year or two. Be patient and happy about small increments of progress, especially if they are continuing to occur.

More Assessment Examples:

♦ **Baseball:** A pitcher wants to throw more strikes. His goal is to throw 2 out of 3 pitches at 95% power as strikes. He commits to practicing for 40 minutes 3 times a week. After a brief run and stretch of 10 minutes the player plans to throw 15 relaxed pitches starting at 50% power and increasing to 80% of his maximum speed (5 minutes). Then he plans to throw 50 pitches, keeping track of balls and strikes at his 95% power level with the goal of throwing 37 strikes. If he throws only 20 strikes he might adjust his goal to 25 for the next session. If he throws 38 strikes he might adjust to throwing the last 10 pitches at 98% of full power or choose to set his goal at 40 strikes. Thus he maintains the challenge level, being certain that he is not just remaining the same, or setting unrealistic goals.

♦ **Hockey:** A hockey player wants to improve his shot. He is already able to hit the two lower corners of the goal 80% of the time within a foot of the post from 30 feet. Now he wants to be able to hit the top corner to within one foot of the post with the same degree of accuracy. He is unable to get ice time for himself but he also has a goal at home. He loves to play the actual game, but commits to practicing his shot with a friend twice a week for a half hour with each of them getting 15 minutes of shooting and 15 minutes of retrieving for the other guy. He sets his goal at 1 in 3 shots because at the moment he is already capable of 1 in 4 attempts. His plan is to be able to raise his percentage 5% for 11 weeks in a row, which he realizes he can raise or lower in accordance with his progress. Once the player starts to think this way you can see how he can progress sooner than by just leaving everything to chance. Naturally, he has to continue to play his regular street and ice hockey, but this focused practiced with a specific goal and assessment is extremely likely to accelerate his improvement; moreover, by adding visualization and imagery, (which are clarified further on), his progress is likely to be even more dramatic.

* **Football:** A running back wants to improve his cuts. He decides the course of 5 yards forward, 45 degree cut right, a 90 degree cut left, forward 5 more yards, then a 45 degree cut left, a 90 degree cut right and ending with 10 yards straight forward has the elements he needs for best improvement. He feels this simulates a very game related successful run. He paints the appropriate marks on his driveway and has his younger brother time him on 5 trials. He repeats 20 of these twice a week with the goal of improving by 1 second every week for five weeks. He notes his progress the second week and adjusts his goal accordingly. He also begins some imagery exercises (see next chapter) in order to feel his good take-off and turns. He constantly adjusts in order to maintain instructional level as opposed to independent or frustration level.

Running backs course for improved cuts and general running and fitness. He started with sneakers in the driveway. Later, to best simulate the game, he starts in a 3-point stance. To further simulate the game, he carries a football. Later, he does it on the kind of turf he normally plays on with his football cleats. To carry it one step further, he could carry a 10 lb weight or even wear his football uniform.

* **Volleyball:** The young lady wants to improve her kills. She has a backyard net with the garage wall behind it for her personal practice. She has decided to self-serve a ball 5 feet in the air, set it about 10 feet in the air and then kill it at the correct moment. In the early stages she finds that she is successful with this procedure 2 times out of 10 trials. She then sets her goal to improve to 3 out of 10 the following week, and to improve by one, every week until she achieves 8 out of 10. The first week she immediately gets to 50% so she changes her goal for the third week to 70% (14 out of 20).

However she fails by quite a bit because, in the beginning, perfecting the basic method was easy, but now progress has slowed considerably. Since she did achieve 55%, she adjusts her goal to 60% in order to stay positive. She arranges to get in the gym and have her season setter serve her for 15 minutes once a week. Her best friend, a cheerleader, is willing to go to the sessions and cheer for her (thus getting some practice in herself) on all her successful attempts, so she is also getting some simulation practice! (Simulation is nothing more than making practice game-related. This topic is covered in Chapter 5.)

+ **Basketball:** The girl, a center, feels that she needs a better turn-around jumper from about 12 feet on both sides of the lane. She tests herself and finds that she is able to sink 3 out of 10. She commits in the off-season to work at home on her own hoop. She also wants to improve her rebounding and put-backs. So she sets her goal at making 4 out of 10 shots, and she wants to catch at least 4 of her rebounds (when she misses) before they hit the ground and make at least 3 put-backs. She works in sets of 10 trials so it is easy to keep track of her progress. Once she is able to hit 60% of her combined shots and put-backs, she feels that she now needs to work with a live defense. She is able to get a younger boy player next door to help her out, in exchange for helping him with his science homework once a week. In six weeks time she notes that she is at a stand-still, so she asks her coach to watch her routine. The coach observes that she is no longer setting up for the shot with deliberation and height because she is too anxious about retrieving the misses. She begins to do some visualization on a deliberate set-up and placing the ball in a true get-set position. She immediately begins to progress again on shots made, interestingly with no down side to retrieving missed shots!

+ For all sports like basketball, involving shots on goal (lacrosse, hockey, field hockey, soccer, team handball, kicking extra points in football): Take 50 foul shots/direct kicks, etc. After every two, jog/skate to the mid-court area and back to the line. If your starting standard was, for example, 30 baskets or 60%, but your last three assessments were 38 of 50, 32 of 50 and 36 of 50, your goal of 80% is not achieved yet, but you are making steady excellent progress!

While examples can be drawn from any number of sports from swimming to bowling to wrestling, the common purpose is to show the high degree of **specificity** that is required in the area of assessment. Also, the close relationship between goal setting and assessment must be noted.

The details of what, who, when, where and how are all important. The amount of time, number of repetitions, and use of equipment (50 tennis balls, 10 volleyballs, access to practice facilities) are details that can foster excellent improvement. Successful people and champions pay special attention to these details as necessary components to their long and short-range goals.

While objective diagnosis is a necessary component to setting and prioritizing goals, a common error is to be overly concerned with weaknesses. Athletes who build on their strengths more often attain excellence and help the team the most. This is particularly true when the weakness involves a relatively minor skill. For example, the soccer player who can dribble and pass with either foot, but can not shoot a rocket with the weaker foot, is like the basketball player who can dribble or pass with either hand, but can not shoot 3-pointers with the weaker hand. These players would do well to build on their assets instead of putting in a great deal of time improving upon a weakness that often can be hidden. Not being able to effectively go left and right would definitely have to be remediated.

Use this space for your notes on your own assessment strategies. Detail the skill and follow it with details on your assessment noting when, where, how much time, with whom, number of repetitions and all necessary details:

_____

_____

_____

_____

_____

_____

_____

_____

27

There are several terms for the concept of "attentional focus rehearsal," but the two most common are visualization and imagery. Visualization is another sports psychology technique that has proven effective in raising performance. It is nothing more than seeing with the mind the particular skill you hope to achieve. Virtually all recent research has shown that five hours of physical practice and one hour of visualization is consistently better than six hours of physical practice! This is especially so when the visualization and physical practice are clearly integrated to one another.

Visualization must be very clear and specific with great attention to detail. A soccer example could be your power instep kick: the vision could be landing on your kicking foot straight in front of where you struck the ball.

Often visualization is aided by a solitary location, possibly a darkened/quiet area with comfortable temperature. You probably need a comfortable posture, relaxed breathing, eyes closed, and high concentration and focus of the desired skill.

There are two ways to visualize. In the first method, you imagine yourself as the actual performer of the act; in other words you are inside your own body as the participant. In the second method, you view in your mind's eye as if you are watching the technique on videotape; in this case you are outside your own body as a spectator. Both methods are effective.

Frequently, when you visualize yourself as the actual performer, the visualization flows into imagery. This term describes visualizations in which the muscles in your body are rehearsing (feeling) what you are seeing. You are not only getting a clear visualization, but you are also getting a physical feeling for the skill.

Unfortunately, the terms visualization and imagery are used interchangeably, though this may not be as absurd as it sounds, since there is likely a gradual difference between the two. Possibly there is a very weak, maybe not even a measurable response, all the way to a very strong measurable response of different intensities. Further research is likely to clarify this in the future.

Imagery can actually improve muscle memory to an even greater extent. In physiological terms you are gaining a neuromuscular response.

Both visualization and imagery must be very detailed. Visualize first in slow motion; then once the technique is perfected, speed up the 'camera' to real time. Focus on the correct way, remain constantly positive, and push anything negative, like poor performance and failure out of your mind as quickly as possible. See yourself performing both your strengths and weaknesses well. Remember, the mind learns from repeated imagery exercises to perform correctly, just as the body learns from repeated physical exercises.

In fact, if there is a skill you want to accomplish that you presently cannot perform, imagery helps you to attain it. For example, if your best high jump is 5'8" visualize the bar at 5'9" and see yourself getting over it cleanly.

Naturally, unrealistic goals connected to your technique or skill will be of little value. For instance, if your best jump is 5'8" at the present time, visualizing clearing 6'8" may be of little value when you go to practice later in the day. However, a year from now, clearing that height could be realistic. Especially if you do serious physical practice combined with imagery. In the space of six months, one such high jumper improved from 6'8" in his senior high school track season to 7'4" in his first semester of college!

Just as a written set of goals clarifies an athlete's various objectives, a written visualization can also be a great aid to improvement. Write out your own exercise for a critical moment in your given sport. You know best what it is that you need to accomplish. Use the space provided.

_____

_____

_____

_____

_____

_____

_____

_____

_____

_____

After you have written your script, rehearse it in your mind while reading it. Then rehearse it with your eyes closed in a very positive atmosphere. Rehearse it several times a day before the event. You may be very surprised at how effective this can be for you. Post your reminder near your bed and review it once in the morning and once before going to bed. These two times are proven by research to be the most effective.

Here the coach is presenting a very positive, vivid guided visualization exercise in order to teach the players how they can do this on their own to improve performance.

In fact, post goals and all your sports psychology techniques regularly on your bedroom wall, bathroom mirror, refrigerator, textbook covers, wherever you are sure to view them. Coaches can use bulletin boards, handouts, and field signs for the same purpose.

Whenever you are having trouble getting started or getting positive imagery, simply think of something wonderful, something beautiful, or something you love. Anything positive (it need not have anything to do with your sport) will help you to move into the sport ideas and skills in a positive natural manner.

Visualization/Imagery Examples:

You are a baseball pitcher and you see the ball's spherical shape in three dimensions. You see the ball's color, texture, exact size, the seam pattern and color, the size of the seam cord, and the ball logo. You step to the rubber mound with your feet comfortable and properly apart.

Your body balance is perfect. You have the ball in your glove and you grip it exactly as you want to for the pitch you are about to throw. In your peripheral vision you see the runner on first base but he provides no distraction to you. You begin your wind-up and your left knee is lifted to your waist and properly bent. As you begin your delivery to the plate, your only thought and your entire visual focus is the exact location where you want the ball to go. Your arm extension is excellent and properly positioned. Your right leg is positioned perfectly for a power push off. You send the ball straight to your target within the strike zone.

You can substitute virtually anything into this framework, whether it be hockey, lacrosse, field hockey, tennis, ping pong, horse shoes, bowling, wrestling, volleyball, football, shooting, casting for fish, or even non-sport objectives such as woodworking skills.

Continuing with the pitching example, you may have a game strategy which is low and away or something varied for each batter, but this is not the time for a lot of concern about the next 30 pitches. Take one at a time. Does this have to be a strike because bases are loaded and the count is 3-2? Then instead of nicking the corner of the plate you may have to put it just below the waist and over the outside half of the plate.

This kind of detail is strategic and is obviously needed. In short, deal with everything that is needed for the moment; deal with nothing else, particularly those long range issues that are not needed for this particular moment. Of course this is easier said than done, but with practice it does become easier.

Another case that happens frequently relates to ice skaters. The skater may be very competent at performing a half turn in the air and continuing backwards. She is also capable of a single turn (360 degrees), so she rehearses mentally a turn and one-half with enormous detail. She also physically perfects the 360 turn with great height to give herself the air time needed for the extra ½ turn. To her great surprise, on her first attempt she makes the one and one-half turn successfully.

Some things you might want to visualize:

Imagine a thorough, effortless, yet rigorous warm-up which allows you to relax, breathe comfortably with your mind completely ready for an excellent contest. In chapter 7, you will learn more about controlled breathing.

See yourself on a fast break with your opponent trailing you; you cut directly to the basket and drop the lay-up softly in even though you got fouled - feel that final sailing step going up to the basket and the ball gently hitting the backboard. Hear the sounds of the footsteps, the crowd, the ball bouncing, the ball swishing through the net. Every one of your senses should be awakened to the action, but most of all you feel your muscles reacting to every single action taken.

Taste your own sweat, smell the opponent, see yourself looking the other lineman right in the eye, feel the relaxed power you have for a great block which is perfectly timed at the snap of the ball; your position under the opponent has given you the full advantage. Be certain to feel the reward of your running back hitting your hole and never getting touched by your opponent. Feel the joy of going into the huddle and having your running back slap your hand in congratulations and knowing exactly what he is saying without words.

See the throw and action of your tennis opponent's service. Hear the ball hit his racket and even though it has great speed your 'slow motion mental camera' gives you time to be positioned for the return as the ball enters your court. See your footwork and full arm stroke return hitting the sweet spot of your racket for a blazing return. Be certain to see your follow through and feel the exhilaration of winning the point.

Visualization works because, after the fundamental stage, one must integrate the physical practice and the mental practice. The rehearsed visualization exercises will take care of the technical details. Concentrating on technical details on game day causes confusion, stress and reduced performance. Game day requires relaxed flow of the entire game or action.

For example, if one has practiced wall passes with all their innuendos of one touch, proper foot position and timing, this is a good time to focus your visualization and imagery on the wall pass. After the details are programmed into the mind, then it is time to view the entire motion at game speed in simple smooth motion focusing on the result.

Another way to understand this technique is to first deal with performance and then to deal with outcome. You do not want to be thinking so broadly that your mind is full of the final score when the game is not even over. Instead, stay focused on the here and now, but not technical details, because those details have already been mastered through physical practice and mental visualization.

Use this space for your visualization exercise. After the first draft, refine it. At a future date, refine it even further:

_____

_____

_____

_____

_____

_____

_____

_____

_____

_____

_____

_____

_____

_____

_____

_____

_____

_____

_____

_____

_____

_____

_____

_____

_____

Research indicates that while all athletes benefit from visualization, imagery and other sports psychology techniques, the more accomplished athlete benefits even further. Conjecture would lead one to believe that they have more skills and so the mental game becomes even more important.

Let's look at another common situation in a basketball game. In the fourth quarter of a close game, a player is sent to the foul line. He has practiced his foul shots in the traditional way, at the end of practice as a winding-down activity with a few of his teammates, while the coaches would discuss players and strategy in the gym office. He could make 65% at practice. But this was show time! He knew the team rule: for every foul shot you miss in a game, you run three laps full speed around the gym. Not recommended, but this was the team rule.

These pressure situations like tournaments, foul shots, penalty kicks, shoot-outs, and the 3/2 pitch at the bottom of the ninth seem to favor the athletes and teams that have "been there before." They have the advantage in dealing with the pressure. So how can you prepare for these situations in practice?

The answer is simulation. Simulation merely seeks to make physical training circumstances as similar as possible to the "real thing." It involves such things as practicing at the field where the game will be played, or with a crowd of spectators instead of the normal practice of just players and coaches, or with a game-like 10-minute interval between the two 45 minute halves of a scrimmage. Blasting loud noise from a recording device as may happen in an actual game, night practice under the lights, or anything that makes the practice experience much more like the game experience is a simulation.

If a coach is generally subdued in practice but very vocal in games, he would simulate his game behavior during a particular practice. If he is quiet and calm at games he would then act this way in the practice before the game. Practicing with the exact gear (uniforms, shin guards, game ball, etc.) would also be simulation, especially in football and hockey.

Why go through all this extra effort? The answer lies in the fact that practice sessions and games are significantly different. Games, of course, add extra stress which athletes must learn to handle in a positive way. But games also add extra distractions, not just crowds of spectators, but perhaps certain spectators whose presence may add pressure or distraction to the team: parents, boyfriends, girlfriends, press, even college coaches and recruiters.

While it is next to impossible to recreate that kind of pressure during any practice session, simulation often works to bridge the gap between the more relaxed atmosphere of practice and the high stress tone of competition. In doing so it helps athletes anticipate and prepare for the next game or match. This is the athletic counterpart to dress rehearsal in the theater world.

But there are other important reasons for simulation. For example, in a typical practice, routine foul shots or penalty kicks offer very little tension. But in a game, these are high pressure situations where all eyes are on the individual performer, and the outcome of the game may hang in the balance. Therefore, the coach should use simulation techniques to recreate the pressure as realistically as possible.

One way that coaches can do this is by insisting that this part of practice be anything but routine. The coach must take it very seriously, prohibiting laughing when a teammate's foul shot or penalty kick is missed. (No one laughs during the game.) There may be consequences for a shot missed at practice, but the coach should use judgment and consider the player's personality; some players may suffer a loss of confidence if they feel that the punishment is too severe or unfairly administered. It is usually best to add just enough tension to simulate the seriousness of these shots. For example, you may want your goalkeeper to kill time just before the penalty kick as a form of simulation.

In these make or break situations during competition, players already feel tremendous pressure. Why add to it by punishing failure or admonishing her that she had better make that foul shot or else? Instead, use a reverse simulation; instead of simulating the game during practice, here simulate a practice instead of the game. In other words, instead of adding pressure, the coach can try to reduce it. Since there is often a time out before that crucial foul shot, the coach can express his confidence in the player's ability and the outcome of the game. How much better would our young foul shooter feel going back to the line if the coach had taken pressure off her by saying something like "I know we're going to win this game whether we make this shot or not. Be relaxed in using your legs to help with the shot, and focus on the rim. Everyone on this bench is with you!"

Of course, the great majority of simulations involve trying to create game-related pressure during practice. Try some of these ideas for simulating various aspects of competition:

- **The length of the game and breaks:** For instance in hockey play three 20-minute periods, in high school basketball play four 8-minute quarters with the standard breaks, with timeouts, etc. In preparation for a televised game, insert the TV breaks so players replicate that situation, or have someone videotape the session.

- **Conditions:** As long as it safe, not lightning and thunder, practice in the rain if games are to be played in such conditions. Using cones, reduce the size of your practice field if your next game is on a small field.

- **Press:** Have members of the school newspaper give a 10 second interview of the players as is sometimes done in the actual game.

- **Officials:** Have an official at practice for the 'scrimmage' portion of the practice.

- **Noise:** Crowd noise and/or piped in music is another common technique.

The list is nearly endless. Obviously it frequently varies from sport to sport. One condition that should be fairly common is to make training as rigorous as the event. Naturally there are light days before events or recovery and over-training days in order to achieve peak fitness. Still, many portions of training should be event-related if you want to have your team totally ready mentally and physically for contests.

Simply stated, focus on the positive notions that have yielded success for you in the past. Avoid long range goals and outcomes and technical details that cause anxiety.

List 10 simulations that you think are the most valuable for maximum achievement:

_____

_____

_____

_____

_____

_____

_____

_____

_____

_____

_____

_____

CHAPTER 5
Focus

As shown in the previous chapter, neither the coach nor the athletes must allow themselves become distracted by the environment. Now let's look at the biggest distraction in many sports. Consider this familiar case: The referee or umpire makes a bad call, or fails to make a call, an ejection or score results, and the entire tenor of the game suddenly changes. The coach screams, the players get angry, spectators heckle, and the game ends in disappointment for the team that suffered that one bad break.

Could such events be prevented? No. Bad calls or bad breaks are part of every sport. That's life. But the results of these bad breaks are not inevitable! When that coach and those players got angry, they lost focus. They stopped giving everything to the game and started giving their attention to something that had already happened and could not be changed. They did not realize that although they could not control the call, they could control their reaction to it. And in many cases, those bad calls or breaks can be overcome.

Players and coaches who get caught up in reacting to the referee, umpire, official, or judge's call are allowing themselves to be taken "out of their game"; they have left the here and now, and have been virtually reduced to spectators or liabilities. This seriously interferes with their game plan and their execution of basic skills.

To prepare players to accept these breaks, coaches must model the appropriate behavior themselves and emphasize the importance of focus for every player.

To train for focus, some coaches deliberately make bad calls in order to prepare players for these eventualities. Combining focus with simulation, the basic tenor of the next game's official may be noted. For example, is this referee going to call every contact or only the more flagrant fouls? Does this particular plate umpire call a larger strike zone than most? This information, though it requires some experience, is useful both in planning and playing the game. It should therefore be used to build, rather than undermine, focus.

Focus is merely keeping oneself fully attentive to the task that needs to be accomplished now. While this can be accomplished, it is not easy. Coaches often observe their players getting distracted during practice and games. Players should monitor themselves just for a few minutes the next time they practice or scrimmage, by asking themselves "How many times did I let my mind wander away from the task at hand?" The answer is sure to be surprising. But no matter how good or bad an athlete's focus may be, it can be improved by the basic psychological facts and techniques mentioned here.

Obviously, nearly all professional, Olympic, All-American, and other accomplished athletes have good focusing skills. Virtually none are so gifted physically that they can succeed on physical skill alone. Most credit the mental skills of sports psychology as the number one component in their success. All of them recognize that positive focus is critical. Great examples of athletes with excellent focus ability are: Jack Nicklaus, Tiger Woods, Fran Tarkenton, Bill Bradley, Joe Montana, Andre Agassi, Mary Lou Retton, Stefi Graf and Reggie Jackson. Race car drivers must have it, or else they risk severe injury or even death. While many great players such as Larry Bird kept constant focus for the entire game, others like Michael Jordan could talk trash and in several seconds refocus and sink his foul shots. Most athletes need continuous focus similar to Larry Bird.

Olympians often prepare months and years in advance, but naturally at practice the focus intensifies as the event approaches. The norm for outstanding younger players is a general level of focus throughout the season, a higher level focus for practice, a further increase the day before the contest, another notch up for the day of the contest, and even higher level focus the last few hours, reaching maximum focus during the contest, especially toward the last minutes.

At practice the details of technique are often the focus; in other words, technique overrides result during practice. But during games, focusing on the results of the entire technique and strategy becomes more important during competition.

Frequently, focus training is begun with a breathing relaxation exercise. Even here, the obvious distractions of environment (weather, field conditions, lighting, etc.) must be dismissed. While the benefits of simulation training in this area have been examined in the previous chapter, here the ability to focus also comes into play. Many start their focus session by trying to picture a completely blank screen, sometimes a yantra (a geometric design used for meditation). Sometimes a simple black page with a white square in the center begins the process. In any case, the object is to achieve a mental state that is free of any distraction.

In a relaxed comfortable position, close your eyes and picture the black of the darkest night imaginable.
Open your eyes and gaze for two minutes until an edge of color forms around the circle.
Look at a blank wall and the image should appear. Hold as long as possible.
When it disappears, imagine it is still there.
After it disappears completely, close your eyes and bring it back.

There are probably dozens of ways to find relaxation, but you must study yourself very carefully and when you find one that works for you, write it down so that you can recreate your focus anytime you feel the need to.

_____

_____

_____

_____

_____

_____

To maintain focus, it is helpful to have a game plan, a specific emphasis, and cue words that serve as reminders. For example, the soccer game plan could be a low pressure defense and counterattacks on the wings. The emphasis could be on denying penetration up the middle, and the cue word could be "inside-out," a code phrase to remind players to contract toward the middle on defense, and expand toward the wings on attack.

The issue of focus is often complicated by the score or time remaining in the game. This may call for a revised tempo, intensity or focus. Such tweaking of the game plan works best when it has been fully employed in practice and it only needs a revision, not a complete overhaul. It is unreasonable to expect to revise tempo, intensity, or focus in a game unless practiced in game-like conditions. Here again, simulation works in tandem with focus.

While there is no simple way to measure the tangible results of focus, experience reveals that those athletes and teams that remain focused win the close games more often than not. In fact, focus may very well prove to be the difference in those games.

Try the following journal entry topics to sharpen your attention focus:

* List the things that most often or most seriously cause you to lose focus.

_____

_____

_____

_____

_____

_____

_____

_____

_____

_____

♦   Make another list of things that will help you to maintain your focus.

_____

_____

_____

_____

_____

_____

_____

_____

_____

_____

_____

_____

_____

A personal experience that I like to share with my players involves a memorable soccer game against our biggest rival. We had a game plan, which included taking advantage of the opponent's tendency to relax a bit whenever the ball went out of bounds. In the second half of a scoreless, hard-fought contest, the play was moving down the flank directly in front of our bench. We all had a clear view of the opponent knocking the ball over the touch line. But the referee awarded the throw-in to the opponent!

Our bench and the crowd of supporters behind them began to protest the call. I quickly reminded my players that their response was not helping, as the opponent casually took the throw-in, and Brian, one of my heads-up forwards, made a tremendous recovery run, beat the intended receiver to the ball, then penetrated past two defenders to score. Had that forward gotten caught up in the spirit of protest, he would never have made that run. The game became ours because Brian refocused before anyone else.

It is every player's and coach's challenge to maintain focus, since any number of things can distract us for even just a moment. A minor collision, a teammate's injury, a hostile crowd of spectators, a miscommunication, a missed opportunity or embarrassing moment, such events happen in every game. They are bound to capture our attention, but we simply need to "get over it," and quickly.

If focus is lost one needs to get back on track by rehearsing and using one or more refocusing cues. A possible cue in response to one of the above negative occurrences, particularly mistakes, would be the word "Cancel!" perhaps accompanied by a suitable gesture, like waving it off or pushing it away, then a positive cue, like "I can take harder collisions than that!"

There are many positive cues useful for refocusing. Words or phases that may help the athlete accomplish this strenuous skill include "Execution," "Extend," "See the ball," "Low & slow," "Stretch." Tactical cues would be words like "Defense," "Cover," "Look left," or "Control."

Cues to instill confidence might include "I can do it," "I feel a score coming," "I can beat my man," "We practiced harder than these guys so we're more prepared," "I deserve success," "I'm fit, so I'm really not tired," "Loose balls are mine," "We've come from behind before and we'll do it again today," "Teams win," etc. And there are always cues that help the athlete overcome anxiety, such as "Trust," "Relax;" "Smile, this is great fun," "Yes I can!"

Any of these can help you refocus and therefore raise your performance. Refocusing is very specific to your sport and needs to fit your individual needs as a player. In addition, they may work differently for different people and various moments. Therefore, you must choose your own cues carefully. They are personal, so they need to be owned by the user to be most effective. Therefore, YOU must create them. In addition to players, coaches also need these same refocusing exercises for themselves, perhaps shortened into one or two words: "Game plan" might be sufficient for the idea that "Our game plan is working," "Our play" may mean that "we know how and when to use this play," "Emotions" is shorthand for "We control our emotions!" "Confidence" can be a code for the coach's belief that "I have confidence in my players."

Personal refocus cues might include "back on track!" indicating that you have stopped a wandering mind to think about the next immediate action. The "here and now" will assist your performance. You may need this cue only once per game; on the other hand you may need to use it over and over again. A marathon runner might use "I feel great!" 50 times or more during a race.

These cues must be used as needed in practice and games. They also need to be simple, ideally a single word or short phrase. Rehearsing these cues in practice allows the simple word or phrase to take on powerful meaning, much more than just the cue word itself. In addition, a deep breath or progressive muscle relaxation can augment the benefits of refocusing.

Think of the five most common distractions that occur to you. Then list a cue word or phrase for each; maybe a single cue word suffices for some or even all of your major distractions. Feel free to revise this at a future date.

	Distraction	Cue Word
1		
2		
3		
4		
5		

Often our lack of focus and inability to perform at peak is as simple as the physical need for oxygen. In the physical realm, aerobic fitness allows for efficient use of oxygen. Without aerobic fitness, our muscles fatigue. Keep in mind, however, that the physical and mental aspects of athletics (and every other area of life) are intertwined and interdependent. The brain needs oxygen even more than the muscles! How many times have athletes, particularly at the high school level, made crucial mental errors late in the game? Aerobic fitness is an asset not only physically, but also mentally, since it helps to keep the brain supplied with that all-important oxygen. Tension and fatigue can affect the delivery of sufficient oxygen to the brain and muscles.

But if we want to take full advantage of the benefits of oxygen, we need more than just aerobic fitness. We need to learn controlled breathing for relaxation. Obviously the unconscious physical act of breathing is generally the same for all people, but the critical part for the athlete is getting additional oxygen and obtaining a calming relaxing response. Nearly everyone who practices these techniques finds them useful. While breathing exercises are partially a natural innate technique, developing controlled breathing can only enhance the value of breathing even further.

Relaxation exercises invariably involve learning how to breathe more rhythmically and deeper in order to get more oxygen to the brain and muscles -- in fact, to the whole body. Sometimes counting the breaths and seeing the chest cavity move may work for you; hearing yourself breathe is effective for many, while taking air in through the nose and releasing through the mouth with sound works well for others.

Some experts claim three parts to breathing for relaxation: 1) intake of air with the stomach coming in and the chest expanding 2) release of air, reducing the chest cavity, and 3) finally the stomach expanding out. Others describe two stages, one for the intake and one for the release. Still others count the moment between breaths as a separate and important step. This can vary from individual to individual, depending on your point of view and what works best for you.

In any case, controlled breathing is certain to increase your intake of oxygen, feeding not only your muscles, but also your brain. This may help you to relax and thereby focus better. By now you are well aware that many of these skills are interrelated, integrated and/or overlap. In this case, relaxation techniques have a close connection to focus.

Simply counting 5-4-3-2-1 slowly is a very effective technique for clearing the mind and relaxing the body. Link it to a deep breath and gain even more results.

Progressive muscle relaxation is the other half of the equation. This also involves the body/mind connection. Here's how it is done: you relax a specific body part, mentally focusing on that particular part, thinking of nothing else but that part, and feeling the relaxation. Then you move on to an adjacent body part. For example, begin thinking about relaxing your toes, then the arch of the foot, and continue up through the ankle area, calf, thigh and finally the abdominal cavity and internal organs.

This technique also works very well for stretching during warm-up activities, where the mental focusing as you stretch specific muscles can augment the stretch, and also alert you to particularly tight areas that need extra time and attention.

It is true, that generally, progressive muscle relaxation is rehearsed at home in a quiet area in a prone or yoga posture and is done in 20-40 or more stages, but a short version can be used during lunch hour or in practice and even games. Warm-ups, time-outs, breaks in action, inactivity in your role or part of the field, are all opportunities to relax more and breathe better. Even a "cleansing breath," a single deep breath exhaled with some force, seems to aid relaxation and focus!

The example above started with the toes and worked up, ending with the abdominal region. Again, personal experimentation with what best suits you is most important. Some start from the scalp, move to the facial parts and then toward the brain and end there. Others start that way and move to the abdomen for the final step. Admittedly the great preponderance of sources start with the lower limbs and work up, but the value of your personal plan will far exceed the "one size fits all" approach.

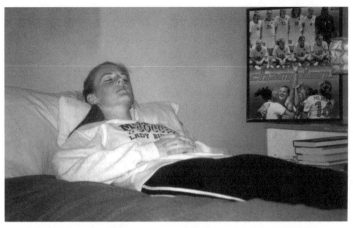

This athlete is working on progressive muscle relaxation (at least that's what we were told).

Create your own exercises, one for breathing and one for muscle relaxation to gain full control of these skills. It would be a good idea after doing the exercise to write it up and then continue to edit/refine it as you continue to use these newly acquired skills.

◆ Using the space below, write an extremely detailed personalized script for your own progressive muscle relaxation. Read it back to yourself several times, fine tuning it to suit your needs. Then record it on a cassette, disc, or any audio device most convenient to your usage. Small portable devices enable you to listen to your script on the team bus, in a car, or around the house. The more numerous the repetitions, the more effective it will be.

_____

_____

_____

_____

_____

_____

_____

_____

_____

_____

53

_____

_____

_____

_____

_____

- After experimentation with controlled breathing, write a script for the most effective format for you. Extreme detail will help make it most useful.

_____

_____

_____

_____

_____

_____

_____

_____

_____

_____

_____

_____

_____

_____

_____

_____

_____

_____

Incorporate a single cue word or phrase with your single cleansing breath during matches. "Feel good", My mind is now clear", "I am energized", "Power", "Release" are among the many you can use. Of course, the best is one you discover after experimentation.

Virtually all athletes have experienced a peak performance, an individual's single best. The plural of this term, often referred to as flow, incorporates the array of best performances. Flow is a relaxed yet focused high-level performance in which the athlete feels he is on automatic pilot, or "in a zone." Flow combines a delicate balance of excitement (not too high or low) and awareness. Physically, the athlete in a zone performs at a high level yet feels little physical exertion. Mentally, the athlete senses both confidence and exhilaration, maintaining focus on the task while avoiding the many possible distractions. There is a feeling of being in full control, yet "letting it happen."

Characteristically, flow involves intrinsic motivation. Athletes who participate for extrinsic reasons may find it difficult to achieve flow. In any case, athletes attain flow only when the challenge is near or somewhat above their present level of performance. Even though the athlete has never performed quite at this level, there is a balance between personal skills and the challenge faced, so that the athlete is ready to step up to this next level. The game plan and hours of practice and conditioning have prepared the athlete for all the physical challenges of the game. But once this is in place, the personal sports psychology training of goal-setting, visualization, focus, and relaxation activities are proven methods of bringing the athlete to that higher level by preparing him for the psychological challenges of the game.

In many ways, experiencing flow can vary with every individual. For most, time seems to slow down, yet they have time to perform at game speed extremely well. Some see the contest as if through a wide-angle lens, while others have a narrow view or close-up of extreme details of the game. A few athletes actually hear a clicking sound when things just seem to "click." Some athletes move in and out of flow during the competition, able to regain it as needed, while others must remain in focus for the entire competition, and possibly hours before.

Flow can have a myriad of causes, but often occurs when a person has a very positive outlook (excellent positive imagery of their required skills) and has relaxed focus. When there are no competing or negative thoughts, self-confidence and self-image are running high.

In addition, any number of situations can contribute to peak performance. For some it is as simple as good food and adequate rest. For others in school it is a matter of dismantling the academic pressure of their education. For extremely low arousal people, flow might occur the rare day when you were really up for the contest. For a high arousal person it might happen on a day where you were a bit tired and as a result relaxed enough to perform at a very high level.

What about you? Possibly the coach you dislike is away, leaving you with the coach you enjoy and who has confidence in you. Or perhaps your father who seldom attends games is there. On the other hand maybe your dad could not attend, and as a result you feel more comfortable. Possibly the players you prefer to play with are all around you today.

Whatever those conditions are, you favor them and/or they favor you. As a serious athlete try to figure out exactly what made you perform well so you can duplicate it in the future. Then you want to write these conditions down in your journal; try to capture every detail so that you can raise your general level of performance and revisit flow experiences on a more regular basis. You probably know some of the causes, and it is likely that you have not yet discovered all the causes.

First list the areas that you know facilitate flow, then list some you think may help you. Finally try, perhaps through meditation, to add at least one more. Attempt to be very specific and clear. Do you think you could join one particular flow experience to a given cause? Again this is an area that you will attempt to perfect. Be certain to write your discoveries in this book, your journal or whatever kind of written record you keep.

Once you know what allows you to have peak performance you can assist it in happening again and again. While no one has ever had a peak performance for every contest, many have gained consistency by discovering the factors that work best for them. The more positive factors that you can identify, the better are your chances of peak performances.

But what about those situations described in the examples above? Your favorite coach, your dad's attendance or absence, and the players you prefer around you? These may be beyond your control, but maybe you can convince your dad that his behavior is interfering with your game. Maybe you can show your coach that you play best when at least one of your pals is near you. If not, then maybe it's time to just let go of that situation and move on to something that you can control, like your relationship with the difficult coach.

Again it is a situation where we use the conscious mind to program the unconscious mind. It would be nice if someone could hand you a formula, but such is not the case. All sports psychology can do for you is to give you insight into what has worked for others and what research has proven.

Generally it is a matter of getting at what drives you most. You may be an individual who sees defeating the opponent as the ultimate success for you. For many, a classy controlled display of their sport is the greatest motivation that propels them to victory. This technique is likely to be excellent for divers, figure skaters and gymnasts, but any individual or team sport athlete can benefit.

Remind yourself that letting go, for many, can be the best way to achieve peak performance. You can control yourself, but not the referee, opponent, or any number of situations. You have great power, but you must focus within, rather than outside of yourself. Self-actualization is in your control; simply seek synergy of mind and body through preparation and practice. Then when it's game time, you can just let it happen!

As in all the techniques, once you get a good start you'll discover more and more of what helps you, and it will get easier with each rehearsal. Whether the techniques are physical or mental, "failing to prepare is preparing to fail." Quality practice mentally as well as physically leads to success. For many the mere mental rehearsal of their best performances just before the game is the best technique. Thus, flow can be enhanced by the techniques of visualization and imagery discussed earlier.

Try using the chart below to help you develop flow in your sport. It might be a good idea to update this chart periodically, perhaps annually, during each season, or even more often.

To a greater or lesser extent, every athlete has had peak performances. Maybe you never quite reached a true flow experience, but by doing these exercises carefully, you will increase your chances immensely.

Recall your best 5 performances	What do you think helped you to achieve excellence on those occasions? Be specific and detailed.
1.	
2.	
3.	
4.	
5.	

While a great deal has been written on the subject, Flow in Sports by Susan A. Jackson and Mihaly Csikszentmilhalye is excellent. Csikszentmilhalye has published several books on the subject of flow; in fact, he is credited with coining the term.

Your own thoughts about flow:

_____

_____

_____

_____

_____

_____

Extrinsic motivation comes from rewards such as trophies and the praise, social acceptance, or approval of others; in other words, factors outside of ourselves, and/or outside of our sport. Intrinsic motivation comes from within the athlete; it includes love of the game and competition against worthy opponents, doing your personal best and not focusing on others, whether they are friends, family, coach or opponents. Research indicates that while extrinsic rewards are not necessarily bad in small doses, when they dominate over intrinsic rewards, performance and/or interest in the sport diminishes. In some cases players may even give up the sport altogether.

By far, the more powerful influence is intrinsic motivation. While there can be a huge variety of reasons for engaging in sport and other extra curricular activities, if passion for the actual activity is not one of your intrinsic reasons for participating, it is often very difficult to perform at the highest levels, even given the natural physical talents to do so.

This team is giving each other Emmy Award Roasts. This team was headed for a playoff game and from past experience the coach knew that his team functioned better when relaxed.

Other teams function best employing headsets with their favorite music.

Long drawn out talks may provide therapy for the coach, but could cause more confusion than assistance for the team.

For many reasons, if you are an athlete with intrinsic motivation, you are more likely to achieve your best, whether in practice or in competition. First of all, physically you are more likely to be in top condition and to have mastered the techniques of your game because you are devoted to the game itself. This enables you to practice beyond your team's minimum requirements. Tactically and psychologically, you are more likely to be completely in the here and now, not focusing on trophies or praise. You are more likely to have practiced visualization and imagery, making you ready for every eventuality.

As an intrinsically-motivated player, you also see the unexpected as a joyful challenge, an opportunity for creation, excitement and exhilaration. You already know that your solution will be a successful one. You simply do not understand how anyone can say, "I can't do it." Your constant attitude is, "I can do it!"

If you are reading this book, then you are likely that intrinsically motivated athlete, or want to be that athlete: reward yourself, play for your own values and your teammates. And believe it or not, if you do your personal best, your friends, family, coach and opponents will recognize your efforts, so you will also get the extrinsic rewards! At the same time your self-image and self-confidence will grow, further feeding your success. Remember that you are the most important controller of high level performance and confidence building.

To help you clarify your motivation for playing your sport(s), try to name two factors that provide the most extrinsic motivation to you, and two factors that give you the most intrinsic motivation. Think carefully about whether each factor is really extrinsic or intrinsic. Do not allow anyone else's factors to enter into your intrinsic motivational factors. Sometimes we find that we are being influenced, or even manipulated by others; the latter is seldom intrinsic motivation. Remember, you are not sharing this with anyone so you can be extremely frank with yourself. Your responses may be a surprise to even yourself now that you have thought about this extensively!

Motivation Chart

	Extrinsic Factors	Intrinsic Factors
1.		
2.		

As Richard Cox maintains, "The motives that young athletes have for participating in youth sport programs are the same motives that lead to the development of intrinsic motivation and self-confidence." These motives include learning new skills, having fun, becoming physically fit, meeting new challenges, enjoying the excitement and the team atmosphere.

Cox's research reveals that "if an athlete comes to believe that an extrinsic reward for participation is more important than the activity itself, then intrinsic motivation will be diminished."

Arousal refers to the degree of a player or team's excitement and stimulation immediately prior to and during competition. Though very important, this psychological concept is far better understood when one has a grasp of visualization, focus, relaxation, flow and similar ideas and techniques. We are all familiar with the phenomenon of "choking" or "freezing" in sports. Coaches and athletes alike are concerned with it, and we have all witnessed it. Choking is often the result of too much or too little arousal; therefore, the more we learn about controlling arousal, the less likely we are to "drop the ball" at crucial moments.

Long before there was scientific proof, most coaches realized that the better performers have better attention focus. This means that they pick out the most important cues in the environment; lesser performers pick out cues of lesser importance. But only recently have scientists examined how arousal levels relate to this phenomenon.

According to Richard Cox, author of *Sport Psychology Concepts and Applications*, "Under conditions of low arousal, the athlete picks up both relevant and irrelevant cues." Relevant cues, of course, are the important events of the game, whereas irrelevant cues are unimportant or distracting aspects in the game or even outside the game. Cox reveals that "the presence of irrelevant cues results in a decrement of perform-ance . . . as arousal increases, the athlete's attention begins to narrow."

For example, in a championship game, a varsity basketball player assigned to guard an opponent man-to-man may follow the ball instead of the opponent. While this player knows better, his total attention on the ball prevents him from staying with his man. His teammates may think that he needs to get more "fired up" but actually he may need to calm down a bit.

The right amount of arousal allows the athlete to focus on the pres-ent game situation. At an optimum level of arousal, irrelevant cues go unnoticed and only the relevant cues remain. The athlete is able to notice the important situations in the game and make good quick deci-sions.

Rainer Martens, author of *Successful Coaching*, maintains that in many team sports like basketball, volleyball, and soccer, performance peaks when arousal is at a moderate level. Cognitive anxiety can overload a player and greatly reduce performance. In the graph below, note how performance is diminished with too much arousal. There is a considerable amount of research to support this idea.

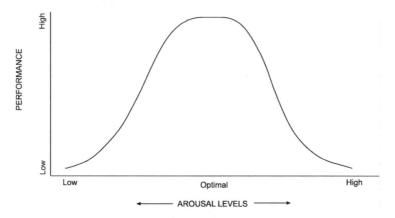

Note how performance is diminished with too much arousal. Cognitive anxiety can overload a player and greatly reduce performance.

Too much arousal is sometimes observable by the athlete's sweaty hands, dilated pupils, and increased breathing and heart rates. In this state, attention may narrow too much, causing one to miss even the relevant cues. How often under the stress of overtime situations have players failed to see the open teammate in position to score the winning point? While this may sometimes be due to fatigue, it is just as likely attributable to over-arousal.

If the notion of too much arousal sounds surprising, it may be because we have been influenced by the popular sports legends, movies and other uninformed media. The typical youth sports film usually portrays underdog teams getting so fired up by a half-time speech that they take the field like stampeding horses and annihilate the bigger and more skillful opponent. Good entertainment, but not realistic.

Another way to understand arousal is through its relation to stress. But in this case, stress should be understood as only part of a word: there is "eustress" as well as "distress." Eustress is essentially good stress; athletes can be taught to understand their pre-game arousal as excitement, a positive condition that will help them to perform at their best. In more scientific language, bodily arousal (somatic state anxiety) to a point is helpful, while distress and mental self-doubt (cognitive anxiety) decrease performance.

With knowledge and practice, it is possible, as well as very important, for players to find that zone of optimal arousal somewhere between the two extremes. Controlling arousal is the final weapon in the sports psychology arsenal.

Since arousal is a very individual aspect of sport, it is, with some exceptions, most often treated on an individual level. While some athletes function well at high levels of arousal, research generally links consistent performance with moderate arousal, as opposed to very low or very high levels of arousal.

Different situations call for varied amounts of arousal. Obviously the team disposition at a given moment in time, whether it be complacency or over arousal (as is common with high rivalry opponents) is a factor in the players or coach's decision regarding arousal. Even within the same sport and team, various degrees of arousal are necessary depending upon team make-up, opponent, league standing, position, and other factors. When playing against a very controlled cognitive team, a team may strive for modest arousal, which allows it to focus on tactics. If the opponent is very physical, a more 'warrior' type arousal may be in order.

For example, a basketball team with superior 3-point scoring might focus on skip passes or penetration with kick-out pass, a tactical strategy requiring moderate arousal. However, against a different opponent capable of shutting down those 3-point shots, the game plan may call for a rugged boards and high pressure defense, necessitating a significant increase in arousal. In the first instance the game plan may more resemble volleyball preparation, and in the latter situation it may be more like football.

In the graph below one sees how arousal is related not only to the

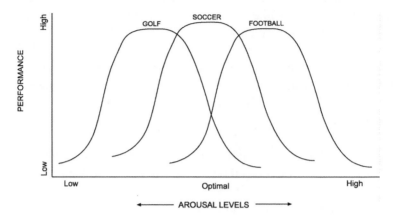

In this graph, we can see how arousal is related not only to the individual, but also to the sporting event.

Possibly the most revealing arousal data is found in Daniel Wann's *Sport Psychology*. The graph below shows the relationship between arousal and task difficulty.

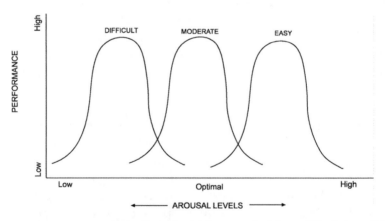

As you can see, an easy task allows for high arousal while a difficult (possibly very cerebral) task is generally performed better with low arousal.

In team sports there may be variations in task difficulty within the same team. For example, in football, the arousal level of the quarterback would have to be much more modulated and cognitive in order for him to make quick, complex decisions. On the other hand, a lineman might require more arousal for a strong, quick hard hit on an opposing lineman. Possibly you can think of better examples regarding a point guard whose role is to 'run' the team and the strong rebounding forward. In any case players need to help themselves find the appropriate level of arousal as opposed to the coach forcefully imposing one level on the entire team.

Since arousal is so variable among athletes, it is best to help them learn about the domain and the ways that they can control their own arousal. The methods of arousal control can involve the relaxation techniques, breathing, visualizations, flow, cue words and even goal setting as discussed in previous chapters. These basic principles of sports psychology can greatly facilitate a player's control of arousal.

The techniques of controlled breathing have been discussed in a previous chapter; now the coach can apply these techniques to the team as a whole in order to modulate arousal. This is especially effective if the majority of players follow up on their own or have successfully used these techniques on their own.

To prepare for this exercise, the team can sit on the floor, ground or bleachers facing the direction with the least distraction. A darkened gym is very well suited to this as well as visualization exercises. Play the excellent audiotape, "Living the Miracle" by Stan Kellner, which is a great program for players at the high school and college levels.

A more personal approach is to conduct your own controlled breathing/controlled arousal session. Try the following script. Talk in a modulated, relaxed tone, the confidence in your voice reflecting the confidence you have in your players:

"Everyone sit down with plenty of room to lie down if that is more comfortable. Close your eyes. Breathe in a deep rhythmically large volume of air through your nose and slowly exhale through your mouth. Find an exaggerated slow rhythm which best suits you. Do this for the next 90 seconds but when we continue with the session, try to maintain

that same slow, deep rhythm. Feel the air entering your nose and moving through the throat area and finally into your lungs. Count slowly to three for intake, then hold the breath for a count of two, and exhale for another count of three. Hear the entering sound and the exhaling all the way through until you take your next breath (remain silent for 90 seconds).

"Now see yourself performing the skill that is most important to you whether it be (skill listed) _____or (another skill listed) _____. Now take another skill which is very team oriented and will allow us to win the game if you execute it perfectly! See every detail. Run the picture in your mind in slow motion, from the very start to the finish. Note your feet, torso and head position as you move through the action with grace and power. (Silence for 60 seconds) Now we are at crunch time and your role either in the game or on the bench is helping us. Everyone is saying positive things to teammates that will help us break the tie and complete an excellent play. The game is over and we have won the game because everyone fulfilled his responsibility. We are in celebration of our success, grateful for our breathing/visualization rehearsal. Now we just want to get on the bus/have a bite to eat/enjoy the moment/go home and have a good night's rest. It doesn't get any better than this!"

Another area of relaxation to control arousal and build confidence at the same time is progressive body parts focus. Everyone is again in a quiet comfortable position, possibly in a semi-darkened area with soft music playing. A small portable cassette player may be convenient.

Try this sample script (use a slow, modulated voice): *"Breathe in a slow comfortable manner and feel the relaxation in the toes of your right foot (wait 15 seconds). Repeat the process with the left foot-(15 seconds). Move your mind to the ball of your right foot and feel it relaxed and joined to the toes. Move into your arch area and feel the muscles in a completely rested feeling (15 seconds). You now feel the heel relaxed and joined to the entire foot (15 seconds). Do the same thing for your left foot (60 seconds). Note how your Achilles already has released the pressure and the relaxation is creeping into your entire ankle area (30 seconds). You can feel your whole calf and shin area becoming loose, and a state of comfort is creeping into your knee (30 seconds). Now your quads are becoming limber, the hamstring area is* *in total relaxation, which will allow your legs to make any movement that the game calls for (30 seconds); now relax the entire buttocks (15 seconds). The feeling of relaxation is creeping into the groin and moving into the lower abdominal cavity (30 seconds). Your chest cavity breathing is at an optimum. You can feel the relaxation of your rhythmical heartbeat moving into the chest and then the neck area and toward your head (30 seconds). The cranial area is joining the rest of your body and your mind has vivid images of your success.(15 seconds) Your mind is in sync with your whole body. Your self-confidence in your abilities as an athlete are at the highest level your can conceive. In fact, you are in total **FLOW!** You feel comfortable about your preparation and fully realize that you can overcome any obstacle. You are a bit surprised that your confidence level is so high, but realize that it should be, since you are relaxed, comfortable and prepared better than your opponents. You know that this rest period will fuel one of your premier performances. Now it is time to let go of everything and simply enjoy the moment! Yes, confidence is a choice, and you know that you made that choice wisely. You feel the aura of your teammates and they simulate your own feelings. This is why you chose sport as one of your recreational activities and have no regrets. You know your experience will carry over to all of your goals. Yes, the here and now has approached a level beyond your dreams and expectations. Let's move on to our game plan (game plan is clarified by the individual or coach): _____."*

The coach can develop a scenario that suits the needs and purposes of the team. Encourage each player to develop a personalized scene that has greater detail, since a hockey goalie has a very different role than a forward. Personal scripting should always be highly detailed to accommodate the specific needs of the particular player.

My best arousal level is:

Physically:	Mentally:

My own script for controlled arousal:

_____

_____

_____

_____

_____

_____

_____

_____

_____

_____

_____

The following grid developed by Russel, Weiss and Mendelsohn, and revised by Raedeke and Stein allows an athlete to evaluate her own arousal and positive/negative feelings. The comparative notion added by the author.

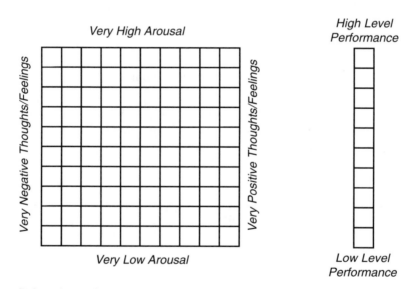

Before the performance, the participant places a single mark in a box to indicate arousal and confidence levels. After 5-10 trials noting the performance after the contest, this becomes very revealing about how to achieve high level perform-ance. Since everyone functions best at different arousal/confidence levels, this method will reveal each player's optimal level.

Just before a game, the player places a mark in the appropriate spot on the arousal diagram indicating her level of arousal; after the game, she places another mark, assessing the level of her performance. By comparing her actual performance quality with her pre-game level of arousal, she can determine when she performs best. As few as four or five games could reveal some insights, but surely after eight or ten evaluations, the information would be much more valuable.

Coming back to the ever-present relationship between the mind and the body, arousal control greatly assists the physical requirements of the game. Recent research indicates that smooth, coordinated sports movements use fewer muscles than awkward movements. Awkward movements use many muscles that are unnecessary and interfere with quality execution. Using fewer muscles obviously reduces the energy required and therefore does not tax breathing and subsequent heartbeat as much.

Relaxation and focus are enhanced. With more efficient movement, the athlete can play more minutes and think more clearly as a result of saved energy. It is definitely a case where less is more. Certainly the relaxed posture and efficient breathing achieved through control of the athlete's arousal level allows this efficiency.

Focus on the basics is another asset to efficiency. One begins to see a congruency between simple and efficient. Of course one may have to spend time on technical details in practice in order to perfect a given skill, but the result of this rehearsal is an excellent performance of everything the body and mind have choreographed.

CHAPTER 11
Positive Affirmations

Affirmations are similar to cue words (discussed in chapter on refocus) but affirmations can be seen as long range items used throughout the year, while cue words are much more related to the here and now, the match or training session of the moment. In other words, affirmations help keep the general course, like preventive medicine, while cue words offer immediate fixes, like first aid. Affirmations can be longer, more complete thoughts, while refocus cue words must be as brief as possible.

In either case, these techniques work because the mind does not know the difference between real and vividly imagined experience. This is why sports psychology is so powerful in improving performance.

All too often, athletes, even experts in the field, spend too much time putting negative things in their minds. But if you quickly replace them with focused relaxed positive input, positive results are yours! Make sure you have fun with your input. Make it a game with yourself to attain results beyond your expectation and those results will be accrued. How could it be positive and not be fun? How could increased performance not be satisfying?

Be certain that your affirmations are totally owned by you, because what you affirm will become a result and a reality. Say, write, and read your positive affirmations several times each day. Tell them to your peers and keep repeating them. At least two to four sessions a day is recommended and is also realistic, since a single minute repeated often can achieve significant results. Most authorities recommend that one these sessions be the first thing in the morning and one at bedtime. Again, significant results will occur withing 4-6 weeks.

Positive affirmations transform our intangible thoughts or beliefs into something firm. Here are some examples:

- I love this sport because it exhilarates my life.
- This is fun! It rounds out my whole life.
- I know it's going in every time I go to the line.
- At least one of our receivers will always get open to catch the pass. I will find him!
- I can beat any opponent on a regular basis.
- No one can return my serves consistently.
- Everything in my game comes to me clearly and easily.
- I can hit the strike pocket consistently, with or without pressure.
- I enjoy and love everything about my sport.
- I am the master; everything I need to succeed is already within me.
- My mind is a perfect channel for creative athleticism and moves.
- I always find myself in the right place at the right time.
- I have so much to give to my teammates when I work hard.
- It's a great gift to be able to not only think positively, but also perform positively.
- I am really an excellent player.
- I feel perfect rhythm.
- I know my affirmations can create greatness in whatever I do.
- My relaxation is so perfect, no wonder I am in perfect flow.
- I completely trust my body to perform perfectly.
- Joe, come back to here and now: This direct kick can make a difference.
- I am a Champion!
- I trust my instincts.
- We can perform at a high level because _____ (every team member randomly completes this statement when he is ready to contribute).
- I will be successful because _____ (complete the statement with any number of reasons; for example, diet, fitness, recovery, training habits, concepts of team, passion for the sport, fun, understanding of one's role, support, vision, goals, values, self-esteem, strength, persistence, consistency, focus, etc. What counts here are values you truly subscribe to and follow up with quality effort).
- I can perform just like I do in my imagery exercises.

Here are some examples for specific sports:

Track: My stride and rhythm are near perfection; I'll cross the finish line first.
Golf: This one is going right to the pin.
Diving: I'll hit the water in perfect form with no splash.
Field Hockey: My stick will always be on the ball first.
Lacrosse (Defenseman): The ball will be in my pocket every time the ball comes near our net.
Swimming: My strength from consistent weight training and laps will make me win.
Wrestling: My new moves are sure to work, even though he won the last two times.
*Mine:*_____

Al McGuire said the most frequently asked question at speaking engagements was: *"What do you say in the huddle with seven seconds on the clock and your team is one point down?"* His reply, ***"Win!"*** Certainly, to some extent this is meant in humor; but McGuire is actually affirming that the team has practiced and trained for this scenario many times. After a brief explanation of the particular option he has chosen, he wants to send his players back onto the floor relaxed. Certainly ***"Win!"*** is the simplest cue word once the option is clarified. It certainly is the most concise affirmation, but like everything else in sport psychology, it is only effective when players are physically and mentally prepared for the situation.

Another important aspect of the physical/mental/emotional connections for athletes involves injuries. Again we see the need to integrate sport psychology with physical training. While the primary treatment of injury is obviously healing and physical rehabilitation, the athlete also needs psychological therapy. Professionals of course have personal trainers take them through a series of physical confidence building exercises to help ensure success. Unfortunately amateur athletes have to learn to develop these programs on their own.

The patient needs to set a goal of daily visualizations, learn a few positive affirmations and possibly a cue word when he starts to drift toward fear or negativism. Naturally the whole array of breathing, muscle relaxation, focus activities and the like will all help the injured athlete to regain full performance.

In many cases the process of rehabilitation can make the athlete better than ever, due to all that she learns about sport psychology. In addition the therapy teaches a great deal about the body and its movements, stretches and exercises, all of which can help in the physical dimensions of the sport. Finally, the recovering athlete can take inspiration and motivation from every great athlete, because virtually all of them at some point in their careers have suffered physical injury or personal setback. In every case, sport psychology techniques, whether inherent or learned, played a major role in their comeback.

Choose your affirmations wisely and use them regularly.

CHAPTER 12
Using Sports Psychology In Your Program

The greatest players and youth/high school coaches teach them-selves/their players to master the basic physical skills of their sport. Attention to the individual athlete's goals, skills and positional responsi-bilities has increased a great deal, especially for higher level play. Sports psychology will not replace those skills, but it will enhance them! This requires knowledge of the game, ability to organize and willingness to prepare. Regarding preparation, John Wooden's famous ratio of two or three hours planning for every hour of training time paid dividends for his individual athletes and the team as a whole. *That's organized!*

Today, the vast majority of practice activities must have clear trans-fer to game pressures. Furthermore, economy of training, activities that integrate technique (basic skills), strategy, psychology and fitness must take precedent. There is not enough time to attempt to do each separate-ly, and again it would be too isolated from the actual game situation. When practice is competitive and game-related, skills transfer to the game.

The history of playgrounds and street ball producing a quality play-er has diminished greatly. While to some extent basketball seems to hang onto this bastion, many professional clubs throughout the world are in the business of dealing with youngsters from age eleven on, and even younger. In some sports such as tennis it appears to be a necessity. Also, clubs in general in organized play are learning about player devel-opment as opposed to merely winning contests, or at least the quality clubs are bent in this direction. Golf, gymnastics, bowling, tennis and a myriad of other sports are frequently employing weight training pro-grams, speed training, plyometrics, sport psychologists, even medical personnel and various kinds of fitness specialists.

Possibly the most relevant idea here is that coaching is becoming a team process requiring many different skills. Still, the youth coach is left to perform all of these roles, not the least important, is sport psy-chology. Lawsuits make it virtually mandatory to replace homespun notions with more objective, scientific methods that can be substantiated with factual data. The ability to clearly identify with the current practice of experts is always a help in convincing parents, community or even a court that one is following safe state of the art practice.

Team building in some rudimentary form has always existed, but now we have access to an array of exciting and new ways of building your team. Numerous books now exist on this topic alone, though comprehensive sources that combine theory and practice for various ages are rare.

In the 1992 Journal of Applied Sports Psychology, Spink proves that high levels of team cohesion are related to lowered state anxiety. He further argues that homogeneity of team cohesion among both starters and nonstarters is an important predictor of successful team performance.

Carron, Spink and Prapavessis in the *1997 Journal of Applied Sports Psychology*, present the following general principles for developing team cohesion:

- Acquaint each player with his/her role and the importance of that role.
- Acquaint each player with the responsibilities of other players.
- As a coach or teacher, take the time to learn something personal about each athlete on the team.
- Develop pride within the sub-units of large teams.
- Develop a feeling of "ownership" among the players.
- Set team goals and take pride in their accomplishments. Challenging but obtainable!
- Do not demand or even expect complete social tranquility, but avoid forming cliques that work against the goals of the team.
- Develop team drills and lead-up games that encourage member cooperation.
- Develop leaders and empower them to help performance.
- Highlight areas of team success, even when the team loses.

Rinus Michels, the world renowned Dutch soccer coach makes a strong case that team building is not achieved by camping trips, pajama parties, canoe trips, field day activities, etc. He regards team building as an intrinsic part of training, of exact role definition, quality training sessions, and crystal clear strategy. He never goes so far as to denigrate some of the extrinsic team building activities, recognizing that many great clubs have a different approach to team building. Michels' psychological ground rules include harmony, rules of conduct on and off the field, team hierarchy, clear objectives, supportive atmosphere, disciplined training camps, and communication.

The importance of communication in sports cannot be overstated. Coaches must repeatedly "get the word out" as to their plans, expectations and philosophy. Messages about goals, focus, relaxation, flow elements, strong visualizations, and perfected methods of breathing can be posted on bulletin boards, at the practice field, on the gym wall, in the weight room, etc. Coaches can give handouts to each player with instructions to post them in strategic places at home or school. The important messages need much repetition, but in many varied ways and with plenty of room for each player to "digest" often enough to own the message.

In spoken communication, individual and team discussions must be part of every practice session and competition. In most cases these discussions are very brief. But real communication is a two-way street. Many coaches would do well to talk less, and listen more! A question instead of telling is frequently in order. An excellent opportunity for listening arises during time-outs and half-times. Players usually arrive at the bench already sharing with each other; their frustrations, triumphs, suggestions, questions, or confusion are very valuable information to the attentive coach.

In team discussions as well as individual conferences, prolonged silence works great for obtaining valuable player input. Like teachers, coaches should practice "wait time" after they ask a question. Allow the players 30 seconds or more, even if it feels awkward at first. This technique shows your players that you really want them to think about and respond to your question, and will elicit more thoughtful discussion.

Another aspect of communication is dealing with the media. This is no time for sharing your concerns about the team's weaknesses. And it is much more than just an opportunity to get the attention of the general public. It is a time to send a message to your players, the booster club and all concerned of your team's assets and possibilities. Share your positive notions and confidence in order to maximize your chances of success. Perhaps you have great team leadership, good defense, great team unity, or powerful academic students. Give credit to those who seldom get much recognition - a strong bench, excellent off season work. If you have a superstar, his statistics are always in print. In that case, it might be best to praise his work ethic, his effectiveness as a team player, or his ability to raise the level of the team during practice and games.

Most of all, be prepared to handle the media situation in a manner that best suits your team's future success. Avoid blaming the referees, and never say anything that would motivate your opponent. In short, let the press help you do the job of communicating and team building.

Accentuating the positive is a remarkably effective technique in every aspect of coaching. Yet players will still make mistakes. One way to reduce the number of mistakes, assuming players have mastered the appropriate skills, is to eliminate the fear of failure. If a keeper gives up a soft goal there is no need to dwell on it or even mention it unless you think she does not know why it happened and how to correct it. Even then, I would probably start with a question to be certain the keeper really didn't understand how the goal was essentially a keeper error rather than a great offensive play. In short avoid the negative, use rewards abundantly, but let the simple truth prevail, in lieu of self-fulfilling prophecy or trying to learn everything through mistakes.

This idea is not in conflict with allowing players to learn through the discovery method. Sometimes the coach needs to see exactly where players are in order to obtain an accurate diagnosis, then proceed with the correct training activities. In other cases the players think they know a given playing strategy and do not. In this case they must be made to realize that they cannot perform it, in order for them to be receptive to learning the strategy. I guess the plain truth is that we must try to make the training program as positive as possible, but there are times in which reality 'therapy' is a necessity.

On every team in every sport, conflicts inevitably arise, and can sometimes be serious enough to undermine your efforts at team building. Both coaches and players are required to resolve these conflicts.

There are many books on this subject; but conflict resolution is generally categorized by five styles, as explained by Bill Sanford of _Team Achievement, Inc._ and Roy Baroff of _Dispute Resolution Services_:

- **Domination:** "My way or the highway!" This approach greatly interferes with high level performance. Players do not learn to think for themselves, and become robotic.
- **Avoidance:** "Conflict, what conflict?" The person who takes this approach tends to not be active in his own performance.
- **Accommodation:** "Whatever you want is okay with me!" Unfortunately in time this frequently festers instead of solving the problem.
- **Compromise:** "Let's make a deal!" This splits the difference, and both sides may win something, but both lose something.
- **Collaboration:** "Let's work it out together!" Only with this approach is it possible that everyone may win, or at least feels good about the solution.

Leadership has been incidentally touched upon several times throughout, and there is no intention again to deal with this topic that is examined in so many good books. Several are listed in the bibliography. Needless to say all engage the notion of vision, delegation of authority, interpersonal relationships, team selection, constant emphasis on problem solving, negotiating conflict, formal and informal power structures, enlisting those affected by the decision in the decision and much more. The point is the coach must be a leader and yield power to assistants and captains who carry out the team mission.

At times captains can be assigned the pre-game talk, often with a general suggestion from the coach or a review of what the captains plan to say. If captains have been empowered these often turn out to be extremely productive. Co-captains and tri-captains often feed off of each other very well in these situations. In any case empowered captains can be very helpful in identifying problems before they get out of hand, even before the coach is aware of the problem. In many cases captains can resolve certain problems more effectively than the coach. This is not done as an abrogation of the coach's responsibilities and leadership role, but as prudent delegation when the coach feels that it is the best way to solve the problem.

One of the notions that I have witnessed to be unsuccessful is for one or two players to attempt to physically carry the whole team. In terms of leadership this may be successful, but in terms of the actual playing this strategy only causes confusion to teammates, and even hard feelings (psychological damage) and is therefore ultimately unsuccessful. Instead, those rare superstars should be trained to "do their job" and encourage teammates to do theirs. A superstar should be treated as someone who lifts the level of the entire team, not someone who tries to do the work of the entire team.

As a general rule the coach selects a system that best suits his personnel. In individual sports, individual strengths are improved and weaknesses alleviated, ideally while respecting the player's individual style. While there are countries, clubs or coaches who have a system they nearly always follow, there is plenty of room for modifications that suit the personnel. Professional and other recruited teams may obtain personnel to fit their system, a luxury usually not afforded to the youth coach. But at most levels, coaches who grow and change outlast those with a rigid system that may be appropriate for only a limited number of years.

In any case it is poor sports psychology to treat one position as more important than another. This may create vulnerable positions that opponents will exploit. It also sets up a poor mental frame when the coach says that the striker, center, quarterback or goalie is the most important position. This is extremely common with goalkeeper clinicians who seem to always claim that this is the most important position. Yet, how much success can a team have that does not score goals, provide service to the strikers, allows many shots on goal, has little offense on the flanks, or simply depends too much on its midfield?

For maximum performance the coach wants to demonstrate that every position on the field has great importance. True, against some opponents, one group may have to do a bit more. But in other conditions, or with other opponents, a different group or individual may have to do more.

In short, make every player and position important to maximize your team performance because this psychology will give the best results over a season or a number of years. Consistency is most often a result of a well-rounded game in individual sports and a well rounded-team in team sports.

This approach also applies to the importance that the coach attaches to each game. Teams naturally "get up" for rivals and championships, but often become complacent about preparing for competition against weaker opponents. The coach can temper these extremes by counteracting the emotional highs of the rivalry and the lows of the weaker opponent. The way to do this is to demonstrate in word and action that the most important game is always the one we are playing or practicing for today. Over the course of the season, each game is important. This is an opportunity to maintain the team's focus!

Another method for dealing with the weaker opponent is to teach your players to work toward individual goals during that competition. For example, the strong shooter can work on assists or defensive play, the power hitter can work on placement, and so forth. Consider this approach not only to keep from running up the score, but also to make the contest of value to your players. Too often, one-sided competition teaches the wrong lessons: the losers feel justified in unsportsmanlike play and are motivated toward future revenge, while the winners feel complacent about easy victories. By avoiding these negatives, the wise coaches teaches his players that being positive and sportsmanlike is a full-time condition.

Of course, the coach has many other duties and responsibilities in order to be successful, but this does not diminish the importance of sports psychology, which is likely to be an integral part of every one of those duties and responsibilities.

SUMMARY

Billy Packer, author of *Why They Win*, interviewed 16 of America's greatest coaches. He asked them a dozen or so questions about the keys to their success. Their responses varied a great deal on all but one point: nearly all thought that the mental/psychological aspect was the most important element of their success.

By now you are well aware that many of the techniques of sports psychology overlap, or maybe a better way to say it is that they must be integrated. Positive imagery facilitates focus and deep breathing, enabling a slower heartbeat and relaxed muscles to perform more efficiently. Therefore, developing any one of the techniques facilitates the development of others and helps your total performance.

In developing these techniques for yourself or your team, the early stages are the most difficult to conquer; but once you begin to see some results you will be encouraged to do more. Your self-confidence and self-image will become stronger. Once that kicks in, your performance can improve enormously, possibly even better than you expected when you started the process.

Any effort to incorporate sports psychology will be of great benefit. Will one or two hours make a difference? Possibly, but significant improvement may entail 10-30 hours of practice. Once your mental training becomes as much a habit as your physical practice, you will be extremely glad you made the effort. Remember always that it will get easier and easier and your performance will reach higher and higher levels. In most cases athletes do not reach their peak physically until 23-29 years of age. But with sports psychology, you can improve many aspects of your game until 50 years of age or more!

Sport psychology parallels sport. In order to become proficient at physical and mental techniques, you must have an abundance of repetition. So practice, practice, and practice some more, and the benefits of sports psychology will pay you dividends beyond your expectations.

Naturally there is an "art" to some portion of sports psychology. Coaches who are enlightened about sports psychology are more likely to be sensitive to their players' needs for recovery, variety, diversion, or plain old rest. We all need time to relax and regain energy and enthusiasm. Sensing this need, coaches may revise their practice plan and substitute perhaps a cross training session or a special low-pressure tournament outside their sport. This strategy often gains a great deal in player motivation.

One-on-one, face-to-face meetings between coach and player may well be the most powerful motivator in sport. That person-to-person touch allows both parties to read the non-verbal communication; most sources estimate that tone, body language, posture, facial expressions, etc. equals 70% or more of any verbal communication. Even five minutes with each player can have great results, especially if it is individualized, personal and well-planned. If time and logistics are a problem, the coach can meet with one player before or after each practice.

The effective coach has **core beliefs**, guiding principles that reflect his values and instill those values into the team. Of course, team core beliefs are also developed by input from players. Instead of "winging" what appears to be the popular idea of the day, review core beliefs every season. Captains can help send the message whenever reminders are needed for newcomers, and forgetful or irritated veterans.

Core beliefs and mission statements provide consistency and purpose so that players gain stability. After all, great individuals and teams by definition are consistent. While all teams have peaks and valleys, sports psychology provides consistency. Highs become less high, and lows become less low. Because the entire team uses positive affirmations, visualizations, focus and relaxation techniques, they can pick up the one or two struggling players. The entire team understands the deep meaning of harmony. It is not a hollow sounding word, but a deep concern of all.

Team building includes an intrinsic style of play, coordination, and commitment (doing whatever is best for the team even when it is painful). The "me, myself and I" approach gives way to the team value: "I pass the ball to whoever is open and wearing the same uniform as me." Affirmations such as, "I will always hit the open player and support her as best I can," can be powerful forces for gaining results.

In short, **team building is part of the style of play, tactics, game plan, and the true meaning of unity**. In this atmosphere there are not selective ranks, pecking order, or favorites; starters and non-starters support each other in practice and competition. "One for all, and all for one" is not merely a hollow slogan; it is living proof as you see the team perform in unison. The ball and game have a beautiful rhythm created by all the movements of the team. A positive chatter and encouragement comes from all members of the team! It resembles a great orchestra bringing its many beautiful sounds together.

Naturally there is an element called talent, but without hard work and intelligent planning, nothing great is accomplished. The flash of insight, serendipity is actually the result of years of quality preparation. In *Sport Psychology from Theory to Practice*, Mark Anshel deals with many training **myths** such as: winning is the only goal, running punishment will make the team fit, pre-game pep talks always help a great deal, coaches need to "cut the players down" to build them up, and if they don't complain, they're happy. Other myths include the value of behaviors like the post-game rampage, the Napoleon Complex, and the use of fear to make them play better. Even a quick read of the previous chapters should make it clear that such practices are negative not only in approach, but in results!

Another myth is that players learn only by doing, therefore brief talks or player responses are not necessary. But the fact is that even professionals and superstars need a reminder or an attitude adjustment now and then. The opposite extreme to "learning only by doing" is explaining everything in detail; this is especially harmful when it is done before every exercise. There are always times when player solutions must be sought or observed, when **discovery** is the best method.

Since we learn by reasoning, imagination, planning ahead, empathy, and seeing different points of view, it is safe to say that we learn from language as well as experience. But if language is used for falsehoods on a regular basis, then the athlete does not know when the coach is "for real," (telling the truth). This is sometimes the case of the self-fulfilling prophecy. In overly simplified terms, the self-fulfilling prophecy is basically a falsehood which undermines the credibility of all the other true and important statements that the coach shares with players. In any case, it is a contradiction to use the self-fulfilling prophecy as a technique to build confidence, and then also say that we can often learn a great deal from mistakes. I subscribe to neither position a great deal. While the coach's job involves reducing errors and poor repetitions, even this should be approached in a positive way. Messages like "Don't move your head or you'll never hit the ball!" sometimes have the opposite of the intended result. Instead try "Nice approach! Remember to keep your head in line with your shoulders as you strike the ball. Then you will hit it with more power and accuracy!" This approach reveals a great deal about the coach's attitude; and attitudes are contagious!

Some coaches do not believe in having a written practice plan on a 3"x 5" card. Perhaps they know their plan thoroughly, or perhaps they are simply rationalizing laziness or arrogance. In either case, Ralph Perez, the assistant to former U.S. National Soccer Team Coach Bob Gansler, makes a lot of sense when he says: "There are no absolutes in soccer." He could have well said in sports, or maybe even in life!

As in all human endeavors there always seems to be at least a little pain for gain, but one should not plan every workout according to this theory. True, there is a need for rigorous work and repetition; fitness training, weight training, skull sessions, and coaching correction are not easy. But teams that plan for success take their medicine without complaint. If the players and coach can put some sugar on the medicine, maybe it can go down in the most delightful way, or at least I like to think so. When players see the value of their rigorous training, they are more likely to accept hard work. In addition, a little humor lightens the load, and characterizes successful teams.

Great players never seem to complain about the countless hours of preparation because they have their priorities in order and are enjoying their participation with the team. Burnout is hardly ever the result of too much sport; it is more often the result of not enough fun, rewards, individual attention, or recognition for the players' effort.

Even the small amount of information presented here would be far better than the afore-mentioned myths, which are based on misguided homespun psychology. Homespun psychology can have dangerous consequences beyond the layperson's imagination. On the other hand, all the values and techniques of enlightened sports psychology are useful for life, for the operating room, the boardroom, schoolroom, home, and for every occupation from butcher, baker and cabinetmaker, to say nothing of becoming a good citizen!

In this way, sports psychology can help athletes make positive choices in every aspect of their lives. One of those choices is confidence. Of course, rigorous physical training can help build confidence. But rigorous mental training completes the picture. Bill Beswick, a renowned sports psychologist, makes a strong case that confidence is a choice. The cumulative result of our choices is our life style. The culture of the professional athlete can seriously affect that life style; big money and fame are often accompanied by pressure and the temptation of negative life style choices. Life in the fast lane has ruined many outstanding athletes.

Even choices that are neither illegal nor immoral, such as poor nutrition, inadequate rest, negative sports psychology and self-image can make success nearly impossible. But children and teenagers have life style problems or concerns of their own. Certainly diet, rest, peer group values, boy/girl relationships, smoking/alcohol/other drugs, inordinate academic pressure, family problems, too much or not enough money are all real problems for any age.

The point of all of this is simple. If life style is such an important factor in performance and in the development of character, values, health of body and mind, how can we take it for granted? Coaches affect the total life of the player in a significant manner. Most say that the mental part is the most significant part of performance and affects the total child. I would think that the coach, since he is the role model and influencer, would want to introduce a sports psychology component into her program.

Goal setting and positive imagery would be a great start. Most coaches should not start counseling in the vital and frightening areas, for fear of doing harm. Yet, if they are practicing the **SCIENCE OF SPORTS PSYCHOLOGY**, all of these areas could be affected significantly in a safe and positive manner. I would go so far as to say that if the coach went to one clinic in regards to youth sports it should be in this domain. In fact there are a few programs way ahead of their times that mandate one session in order to coach. Nearly all high school coaching certifications require sessions on sport psychology.

Unfortunately, those clubs are an extremely small minority at the present time. Possibly the hope of amateur volunteers achieving these grandiose notions is totally unrealistic. I think not. Is the answer to do away with amateurs? No, but anyone who can spend several hundred hours with the children at practice, games, and tournaments can certainly find two or three hours to make the other hundreds of hours more productive.

What if sports psychology training for coaches were made mandatory by law or league rule? I personally think we would not lose many coaches, because virtually all would comply if it were a requirement. Furthermore, if we had 10% fewer coaches, but 90% were better qualified, how can that be a net loss?

There is much more to sport psychology than this little introduction, but as the title reveals, these are the basics. Athletes as well as coaches should be encouraged to do further investigation. Books abound, though few list the activities needed by the coach. Websites are numerous, though most are trying to sell something that is quite expensive. But many coaches would be capable of initiating a one or two hour session on the science of sport psychology; some may even be capable of doing an hour just on goal setting and how players should set up their personal journals.

There may be other valuable sources, but my search led me to these. For certain the near future will produce more and even better materials, but I feel that the Newton explanation holds true: "It is not I, but the great men's shoulders that I stood upon that allows me to see further." While I make no claim to see further I hope to provide simple, concise, and clear information, useful for every athlete and coach. Future authors may be grateful for the authors mentioned in the text and listed in the bibliography, and pioneers such as Thomas Tutko and Alan Goldberg. I certainly appreciate the great work of all, especially seminars with Bill Beswick and Colleen Hacker.

Sports psychology offers a great opportunity in an enjoyable environment for a richer and more fulfilling life. As a player striving for excellence in sport, realize that even if you never make a living from it, you may enjoy it recreationally with great benefits to your health and happiness. Furthermore, your experience will carry over to all that you do in your life, not the least being your family life and future occupation. As a coach these same rewards will be augmented by the satisfaction of bringing out the best in dozens, perhaps hundreds, of young athletes. Many of them will pass these lessons on to future generations.

Enjoy the process and the journey, because learning and growth are the essence of life!

Write a summary of all the major points you have learned throughout the entire text. An alternative is to do a summary of your major goals, visualization scenarios, assessments, focusing techniques, cue words etc. Possibly you have decided to do both.

_____
_____
_____
_____
_____
_____
_____
_____
_____
_____
_____
_____
_____
_____
_____
_____
_____
_____
_____
_____
_____

Extensive warm up is always important. Being "warmed up" is characterized by increased heart rate, heavy breathing and sweating. The latest information de-emphasizes pre-game stretching and emphasizes post game stretching, which is valuable for extending the range of motion and reducing muscle soreness. This is so because the body is truly warmed up at the end of practice or a game. For a long time it has been known that ballistic stretching can cause sprains and therefore is to be avoided. Static stretching was encouraged for a long time in spite of lack of evidence of its usefulness, but has been found to cause muscle laxity which reduces power and thereby performance. Dynamic stretching is encouraged and can best be understood as taking giant steps and holding for about 5 seconds. Stretching should progress from large to small muscles. Pre-game stretching is still used more as a psychological tool since many players are in the habit of doing it and think it prevents injury, though research does not confirm this. In short, keep pre-game stretching to a minimum; very light and short in total time duration. Stretching is still used in therapy with some success. Older individuals may also find it very useful.

This is a very new area of knowledge and we are certain to learn much more about it in the next decade, though as in all cases, due to the information lag, it may take much longer to see a big change in practice. See the article by Dr. Bob O'Connor of Oslo, Norway in *Coach and Athletic Director Magazine, January 2003.*

Note: a "sports psychology" engine search on the web yields a great deal of information

Ansel, Mark H. *Sport Psychology from Theory to Practice*
Baroff, Roy. *www.roybaroffmediation.com*
Bender, Sheila. *Keeping a Journal You Love*, book
Bennett, James & James Pravitz. *Profile of a Winner*, book
Beswick, Bill. *Focused for Soccer*, book
Carroll, Jim. *The Basketball Diaries*. New York: Penguin Books, 1987
Carron, Spink & Prapavessis. *Journal of Applied Sports Psychology 1997*, journal
Cox, Richard H. *Sport Psychology Concepts & Applications*, outstanding textbook with substantial annotated research
Fulwiler, Toby. *"Journals across the Disciplines."* December 1980
Garfield, Charles. *Peak Performance*, book
Gawain, Shakti. *Creative Visualization*, book
Goldberg, Alan & Dan Gaspar. *"The Psychology of Winning Soccer"*, audiocassette
Harris, Bette & Dorothy Harris. *The Athlete's Guide to Sports Psychology*, book
Hershberg, Samuel. *http://www.Mindtools.com*, website
info@mentalstrength.com, website
Jackson, Susan A. & Mihaly Csikszentmihaly. *Flow in Sports*, book
Kellner, Stan. *"Living the Miracle"*, book, audiocassette
Loehr, ...*The New Toughness Training for Sports*, book
Martens, Rainer. *Successful Coaching*, book
Orlick, Terry. *Psyching for Sport*, book
Packer, Billy. *Why They Win*, book
Porter, Kay & Judy Foster. *The Mental Athlete*, book
Sanford, William. *www.teamachievement.com*
Seefeldt, Vern, Editor. *Handbook for Youth Sports Coaches*, book
Sommer, Bobbe. *Psycho-Cybernetics 2000, Maxwell Maltz Foundation*
Thompson, Jim. *Positive Coaching*, book
Ungerleider, Steven. *Mental Training for Peak Performance*, book
Useem, Michael. *The Leadership Moment*, book
Wann, Daniel. *Sport Psychology*, book

Warren, William E. *Coaching & Motivation: A Practical Guide to Maximum Athletic Performance.* Reedswain, 1983

Wooden, John. *They Call Me Coach*, book

ABOUT THE AUTHORS

Andrew Caruso has coached boy's high school varsity basketball and girl's varsity soccer as well as over 25 years of club athletics in baseball and other sports. He has coached ages five through adult for both men and women in three sports, including state teams and was a staff member of Olympic Development Program in New York, Pennsylvania and Florida for soccer. He holds an A License in soccer as well as all the National Soccer Coaches of America licenses including the Residential Youth License and Premier Certifications.

The founder and former President of Kwik Goal Ltd. enriched his background by working with thousands of athletic directors and coaches in all sports for sixteen years.

An educator for twenty-six years including K-12 teaching, supervising, and administrating, Andrew's awards include Teacher of the Year and the Simon Sherman Award for the United States by the Soccer Industry Council of America in 1996. He has always been an active civic leader in his community. He has published over 100 articles on sport and three books on soccer as well as booklets on First Aide and baseball.

An avid gardener, reader, golfer, fisherman, Andrew continues to coach high school and club ball.

Richard Diedrichsen has been an integral part of Andrew's publishing since the beginning. His awards include Coach of the Year and Who's Who in Education; his teams have won sportsmanship awards on the state and regional level. A teacher, coach and parent, he has coached and promoted soccer in Connecticut at the youth, high school and adult levels. Richard's advanced editing and organizational skills add much to this effort.

The authors want nothing more than to place these practical ideas into the hands of the many coaches who seek a simple and practical source in this critical area.